The Road to

Critical Studies on Islam

Series Editors: Azza Karam (Director of the Women's Programme at the World Conference on Religion and Peace, New York) and Ziauddin Sardar (Editor of the critical international journal of contemporary art and culture, *Third Text*)

The Road to Al-Qaeda

The Story of bin Lāden's
Right-Hand Man

Montasser al-Zayyāt

Introduction by Ibrahim M. Abu-Rabi'
Translated by Ahmed Fekry
Edited by Sara Nimis

Pluto Press

LONDON • ANN ARBOR, MI

First published by Dar Misr al-Mahrusa, Cairo, 2002; second edition published
by Ula al-Nahiy for Media Production, Cairo, 2002.

This edition published 2004 by Pluto Press
345 Archway Road, London N6 5AA
and 839 Greene Street, Ann Arbor, MI 48106, USA

www.plutobooks.com

British Library Cataloguing in Publication Data
A catalogue record for this book is available from the British Library

ISBN   0 7453 2176 3 hardback
ISBN   0 7453 2175 5 paperback

Library of Congress Cataloging in Publication Data applied for

10   9   8   7   6   5   4   3   2

Designed and produced for Pluto Press by
Chase Publishing Services, Fortescue, Sidmouth, EX10 9QG, England
Typeset from disk by Stanford DTP Services, Northampton, England
Printed and bound in Canada by Transcontinental Printing

Contents

Series Preface

Critical Studies on Islam
Series editors: Azza Karam
and Ziauddin Sardar

Islam is a complex, ambiguous term. Conventionally it has been used to describe religion, history, culture, civilization and worldview of Muslims. But it is also impregnated with stereotypes and postmodern notions of identity and boundaries. The diversity of Muslim peoples, cultures, and interpretations, with their baggage of colonial history and postcolonial present, has transformed Islam into a powerful global force.

This unique series presents a far-reaching, critical perspective on Islam. It analyses the diversity and complexity of Islam through the eyes of people who live by it. Provocative and thoughtful works by established as well as younger scholars will examine Islamic movements, the multilayered questions of Muslim identity, the transnational trends of political Islam, the specter of ethnic conflict, the political economy of Muslim societies and the impact of Islam and Muslims on the West.

The series is built around two fundamental questions. How are Muslims living, thinking and breathing Islam? And how are they rethinking and reformulating it and shaping and reshaping the global agendas and discourses?

As Critical Studies on Islam seeks to bridge the gap between academia and decision-making environments, it will be of particular value to policy makers, politicians, journalists and activists, as well as academics.

Dr Azza Karam is a Program Director at the World Conference of Religions for Peace (WCRP) International Secretariat based in New York. She has worked as a consultant and trainer with the United

Nations and various Middle Eastern and European NGOs, and has lectured and published extensively on conflict, Islam, the Middle East and the politics of development issues. Her books include *Women, Islamisms and State: Contemporary Feminisms in Egypt* (1998), *A Woman's Place: Religious Women as Public Actors* (ed.) (2002) and *Transnational Political Islam: Religion, Ideology and Power* (2003).

Ziauddin Sardar is a well-known writer, broadcaster and cultural critic. He is the editor of the critical international journal of contemporary art and culture *Third Text* and considered a pioneering writer on Islam. He is the author of several books for Pluto Press, most recently *Islam, Postmodernism and Other Futures: A Ziauddin Sardar Reader*, edited by Sohail Inayatullah and Gail Boxwell.

Notes on the English Language Edition

Ahmed Fekry and Sara Nimis

Spellings for Arabic names and words in this text are chosen to facilitate easy pronunciation and reading for the English reader, without bogging him or her down with phonetic symbols. For this reason we have used the English equivalents for those consonants in the Arabic language that have close equivalents in English. Two consonants that have no close equivalents are the *'ein*, a voiced pharyngeal fricative sound represented in the text by an / ' / and the *hamza* or glottal stop which is represented by an / ' /. Arabic also has a system of long and short vowel sounds, which is a useful guide for stressing the correct syllable in a given word. The long vowel sounds are represented as /ee/, /ū/ and /ā/.

Terms and names specific to Egypt are spelled to reflect their local pronunciation, most noticeable in the use of 'g' (in names such as the Gamā'a al-Islāmiyya) where a classical pronunciation would call for a 'j'. In less regionally specific (usually religious terms), such as *jihādi*, the spelling reflects the classical pronunciation. For names that are well known in the English press, or that have official English spellings in Egypt common spellings are used. For example, Al-Qaeda rather than Al-Qa'da.

The following are Arabic terms that do not have an English translation that sufficiently captures their meaning in Arabic. Terms in italics are transliterated using the above system, whereas terms in normal print have a standard English spelling.

1. *ameer*: literally "prince," refers in the text to the leader of an Islamist group

2. *ansār:* historically the inhabitants of Medina who supported the Prophet upon his arrival in their city after his migration from Mecca

3. *awqāf:* religious endowments which go to support mosques and other religious institutions

4. *azhari:* a graduate of the Al-Azhar University in Cairo, a Sunni institution which draws students from all over the Muslim world

5. caliph: from the Arabic *khalifa,* refers to political and spiritual leader of the greater community of Muslims

6. caliphate: the lands falling under the authority of a caliph

7. *da'wa:* literally "call" or invitation", refers to the efforts of pious Muslims to bring other Muslims to a life guided by Islamic orthodoxy

8. *fatwa:* an authoritative command or proclamation regarding a religious question, issued by a scholar of Islamic *fiqh* (below)

9. *fitnah:* literally "ordeal," refers to civil strife, or more specifically to fighting between political factions with ideological differences, such as in the time after the death of the Prophet

10. *fiqh:* the science of Islamic law

11. *hadeeth:* The traditions of the Prophet, including his habits and the sayings attributed to him. For Sunni Muslims these traditions are an important component of Islamic *shari'a*

12. hajj: the obligatory pilgrimage to Mecca, which all Muslims should perform within their lifetime; also used as a term of respect for one who has completed the pilgrimage

13. *halāl:* acceptable according to Islamic law or Islamic *shari'a*

14. *harām:* forbidden according to Islamic law or Islamic *shari'a*

15. *hijra:* literally "migration," refers to the migration of the Prophet to Medina, or more generally, to Muslims leaving communities of nonbelievers

16. *ijtihād:* the use of independent judgment as a source of knowledge

17. Islamic: associated with or having the characteristics of the religion of Islam

18. Islamist: person or organization actively promoting the application of Islamic principals to the political sphere

19. jihad: literally "struggle" or "battle," refers to the duty of all Muslims to struggle against wrongfulness and fight those who threaten Islam

20. *jihādi*: supportive of or promoting the importance of jihad; in the text it refers to those supportive of militant action to achieve Islamist goals

21. Koran: The holy book of Islam

22. *muhājireen*: literally "migrants," originally refers to those who followed the Prophet in his migration from Mecca to Medina. The term is also used in the text to refer to the Arab Afghans, or Arabs from various countries who moved to Afghanistan to participate in jihad

23. *mujāhideen*: Those who are fighting jihad. In the text refers to those fighting the Soviets in Afghanistan

24. *'omra*: a minor pilgrimage

25. *redda*: literally "to turn away," refers to conversion from Islam to another faith, or ceasing to believe in the tenets of Islam

26. *shari'a*: literally the Islamic "path," refers to the guidelines by which good Muslims should live

27. *shura* council: high level decision-making body in Islamic organizations and governments which takes decisions through consensus

28. *sunna*: prophetic traditions, including habits and sayings attributed to him

29. Sunni Muslims: Muslims who derive their understanding of Islamic *shari'a* from the *sunna* or traditions of the Prophet. The majority of the world's Muslims are Sunni

30. *umma*: The Islamic nation or community of believers, the greater nation of all Muslims. Originally referred to the followers of the Prophet, now is also used to mean nation generally

The translators have added explanations of regionally specific references to the original Arabic version. This material is found in the text in brackets, and in the endnotes.

Preface

Montasser al-Zayyāt's critical biography of Ayman al-Zawahiri is an important resource for unlocking the mysteries of the Al-Qaeda organization, and the international Islamist movement. Zawahiri is today one of the most wanted people in the world, known as the second in command in the Al-Qaeda organization after Osāma bin Lāden. He is considered by some experts to be the brains behind its operations. It is significant that an Egyptian has taken this role. Egypt has a long history of both forceful modernization schemes, and fierce resistance to them, usually charged with an Islamist ideology. Egyptian Islamists are numerous and have much experience in the strategies of confronting the powers that be. Zayyāt's writing is both a psychological biography of Ayman al-Zawahiri and a history of the Islamist movement in Egypt, both of which were pivotal in the development of Al-Qaeda. Thus, the book gives a unique insider's view into the pressing questions of the origins of the Al-Qaeda organization, its objectives and strategies, and what should be expected from it adherents in the twenty-first century.

Montasser al-Zayyāt's status as an insider to the Islamic movement in Egypt dates back to 1975 when the movement was gaining new popularity among Egypt's youth. He first met Ayman al-Zawahiri when he was imprisoned by the Egyptian authorities in 1981 as a suspect in the assassination of then Egyptian president, Anwar al-Sadāt. His historical project expanded upon publication of Ayman al-Zawahiri's book *Knights Under the Banner of the Prophet*, which was written somewhere in the caves near Tora Bora during the American strikes on Afghanistan, then published in December of 2001. Zawahiri's book contained ideological rants and stinging critiques and accusations of Zayyāt and others. Zayyāt addresses many of those ideas and accusations in his writing.

The publication of the original Arabic version of Zayyāt's history and response to Zawahiri in 2002 was surrounded by some controversy from its Egyptian readership. Zayyāt emphasizes that this was not due to any disagreement regarding the validity of the information contained in it. Rather, some Islamists disagreed with the timing of the book, because it was published during the United States military strikes against Afghanistan. Egyptian Islamists saw the strikes as unjust and in the service of cynical American interests. They feared that the criticisms in the book would serve to justify American aggression. For this reason, Zayyāt decided not to print a second edition in Arabic.

The English version of Zayyāt's book comes at a critical time, when Ayman al-Zawahiri is coming to the fore as the deputy head of the Al-Qaeda organization. In January of 2003, Zawahiri sent an email to the website of Zayyāt's organization, the Future Center for Studies, praising the September 11 attacks, and issuing what the *Cairo Times* called a "cyber call" for continuing attacks against Americans (January 16–22, 2003). Zayyāt's close relationship with Zawahiri in earlier days, and his continued contact with him, makes his psychological biography of Zawahiri a key piece in understanding not only the philosophy of the second most wanted man in the world, but the general phenomenon of militant Islamism and the new trend toward targeting the United States and its allies.

As a history of Islamist movements in Egypt, Zayyāt's book is an important resource for English language readers and researchers who are interested in the details of the activities of the various Islamist groups in Egypt. Because of the repressive political environment in which they function, and the resulting secrecy of these organizations, even experts on the subject are deeply confused about the dynamics of the multiple organizations that make up the movement. As an insider, Zayyāt has become an invaluable resource for Western academics and journalists seeking a deeper understanding of the issues at stake.

Islamism

Islam has many contemporary forms, sects and offshoots. Ideas of what the "true" Islam is in this day and age vary greatly among the different groups. Only a minority of believers in Islam (Muslims) are also proponents of the modern political philosophy that has come to be called Islamism. This political philosophy can be defined in the broadest sense as one promoting the application of Islamic *shari'a* (Islamic principles) to modern governance. Within the Islamist movement, there are many divisions regarding not only the structure and nature of the ideal Islamic government, but also the appropriate means for achieving it. Below is a brief overview of the tenets that are common to most Islamist groups, and that distinguish them from the general population of Muslims, as well as some of the main points of disagreement among Islamists.

In the Islamic tradition, the Prophet himself, along with some close companions who ruled after him, was a political, military and economic leader. According to this tradition, it was this leadership, guided by a prophetic understanding of divine justice, which enabled the wealth and greatness of the Islamic empire to emerge from the harshness of life in the war zone that was the Arabian peninsula in the time of *jahiliyya* (literally "ignorance"), meaning paganism. For this reason, a fundamental unifying idea among Islamists is that Islam is not only a way of life, but a way of just leadership in the spheres of politics and economics. Thus, for Islamists, real Islam is not possible under secular leadership.

It is from this vision of their history that Islamists understand political rule by Islamic *shari'a* to be the only guarantor of prosperity and harmony on earth, and paradise after death. The military weakness and economic hardships of people of the Muslim world, through the colonial period to the present, are attributed by Islamists, as well as much of the general population, to the error of following Western hegemony instead of Islamic *shari'a*. This history of defining good politics through religious reference has infused Islam with a distinctly political character throughout its historical development. Faith in the benefits that would flow from government in the tradition of the Prophet is at the root of Islamist intolerance for national policies that are controlled by a dependence upon American aid, or by the need to maintain good trade relations. The most often cited example of the folly of bowing to American pressures in regional politics is the situation of the civilian population in the Palestinian territories. Television news in the Arab world is flooded with pictures of Palestinian women and children, unprotected by any army, throwing themselves bodily against the Israeli tanks that continue every day to roll into new neighborhoods.

While most Muslims would agree that Western hegemony has produced a sad state of affairs in the Arab world, Islamists are distinguished from the general population by their beliefs about what is the practical and correct response. In Egypt, Muslims can be divided roughly into three groups in terms of their perspectives on the appropriate response to the present situation of political disempowerment in the Arab world: mainstream Muslims, Islamists who support what they call a *da'wa* approach to social transformation, and Islamists who support a *jihādi* approach.

As stated above, most mainstream Muslims generally agree with the complaints that more radical Islamists have against American hegemony. However, unlike Islamists, most Muslims consider direct confrontation with the powers that be as something to be avoided. Their reasons range from a strong preference for peace and stability to a sense of weakness in the face of international power politics. Besides a general resistance to resorting to armed struggle among mainstream Muslims, there is a clear consensus that attacks against civilians are *harām*, or forbidden by Islam. One reason for this position is that most Muslims assume that American citizens are not directly responsible for the harmful or unjust activities of their government. Even for those who do blame the American public for the country's unfair foreign policies, almost all Muslims agree that the prophetic traditions clearly forbid attacks against civilians under any circumstances.

Islamists are distinguished from mainstream Muslims because they are politically active in promoting a government based on Islamic principals. Islamists who believe in using the *da'wa* approach seek to achieve social change through a bottom-up approach. The term *da'wa* means literally "calling" and refers to the practice of Muslims calling others to the right path, or a life guided by Islamic orthodoxy. Based on an Islamic principle that advises Muslims to begin social change with themselves, these activists work to live a good life, and to spread their ideas through their communities, hoping eventually to create an Islamic state by transforming the population at large into a pious community. The Muslim Brotherhood in Egypt is the most well-known contemporary organization concerned with the *da'wa* approach, though many more exist. The most direct participation that members of this organization take in impacting government policy is to run for seats in the People's Assembly as independent candidates (the Brotherhood is outlawed as a political party in Egypt). There is general agreement among Islamists who follow a *da'wa* approach that it is *harām*, or forbidden by Islam, to target civilians of any nationality or religion.

Jihādi Islamists are the minority within the Islamist movement who believe in a militant approach to social change. They seek to transform Muslim societies from the top by fighting leaders who use political power to lead Muslims away from the path of righteousness. Their goals are generally to eliminate the Western influence in the region and reclaim the governance of areas already populated with a Muslim majority for Muslims who intend to rule by Islamic *shari'a*. In earlier stages, *jihādi* organizations tended to target key military or official personnel in local modernizing regimes and not civilians. There is a recent trend, however, toward shifting targets from local Western-oriented institutions toward the Western power centers themselves.

Jihādi groups such as Zawahiri's Egyptian Islamic Jihad and the Gamā'a al-Islāmiyya found much support among *jihādi* Islamists for armed strikes on military and government personnel. Still, the question of attacks against civilians remains a sticky point in the ideology even of these groups. As will be described in the following chapters, to whatever degree civilians, Egyptian or foreign, became the targets or accidental victims of these attacks, *jihādi* groups witnessed a corresponding decline in their popularity. The Luxor attacks perpetrated by the Gamā'a al-Islāmiyya led to internal divisions in the group and eventually to its famous ceasefire initiative, in which Zayyāt was a key player. Still, the issue continues to be a source of controversy and disputes even within the most militant groups. The multiplicity of perspectives among *jihādi* Islamists, coupled with the sense that any ideological deviation is *harām*, or forbidden, has assured the continued splintering of groups and breaking of alliances.

Osāma bin Lāden distinguished himself and the Al-Qaeda organization from many *jihādi* Islamists on the questions of targeting civilians and targeting the West when, in February of 1998, he issued a *fatwa*, or a religious judgment meant to be binding on all Muslims (published in its entirety by *Al-Quds al-'Arabi* in Arabic), calling for continued attacks against Americans anywhere in the world. He justified his call with the argument that civilians in the United States and other allied countries use their tax dollars to support policies that have led to the deaths of Muslim civilians, and that for this reason they can be considered combatants. Perhaps the most important function of the Al-Qaeda organization is its ability to manage the divisions between *jihādi* groups, and internationalize the *jihādi* movement into one unified organization made of discrete units each with its own leadership. The characteristics unique to the Al-Qaeda organization are discussed in greater detail below.

Developments in ideology and strategy

Zayyāt brings out several turning points in the development of the ideology and strategy of Dr. Zawahiri that have important implications for the phenomenon of militant Islam in general. Zayyāt points to the death of the Egyptian activist Sayyid Qutb as an event that had a deep impact on Zawahiri and other young Egyptians, who were disgruntled with what the revolution had brought them. Qutb was famous for his book *Milestones* in which he charged modern Muslim regimes with *jahiliyya*, or the ignorance of being non-Muslim. He argued that modern institutions and ideologies were innovations to be rejected as a whole and that Islamic *shari'a*, as a divinely dictated way of life, should be implemented in its completeness. Zawahiri, like many young Egyptians, was drawn to Islamism when the Nasser government made a martyr of Qutb by putting him to death by hanging on August 29, 1966 for his radical views. Qutb's guidelines for activists are seen by many Islamists to be the foundation of the contemporary movement.

Zayyāt describes Zawahiri's experience of torture at the hands of the Egyptian authorities after the assassination of Sadāt as a devastating blow in Zawahiri's life. In his account, the Zawahiri that lived in Egypt, before the torture that led to his flight to Saudi Arabia, is a soft-spoken, modest and thoughtful person. There are many indications that the radicalization of Zawahiri, which has landed him in his present situation as an international outlaw, developed after his experience of torture at the hands of the Egyptian regime. Torture was and still is considered by the Egyptian authorities as a means of fighting terrorism: it is effective in eliciting information from suspects regarding possible future attacks, and in apprehending other activists. According to an article in the *Guardian*, issued January 24, 2003, many human rights activist have observed the link between the humiliation and trauma of torture, and militant political activity. This element of Zayyāt's narration deserves special attention as a clue to the sources of the general phenomenon of militant activity, especially in reference to the Islamist movement.

Another important shift that Zayyāt's narrative witnesses in Zawahiri's ideology is the changing of the focus of verbal and military attacks from local regimes to the international system, and more specifically its main power center in Washington. A few decades ago, many Islamic groups were struggling against what Zawahiri named the "near enemy," meaning governments consisting primarily of Muslims ruling a Muslim majority, but using Western institutions and cultural forms. These have lost credibility among Islamists, usually due to their accommodation of the interests of their Western allies, many of whose policies appear to be biased against the interests of the masses in the region. These are enemies because they are unable to rule by the requirements of Islamic *shari'a*, and because they appear to be cynically uninterested in the opinions of their people.

It was believed that the goals of eliminating foreign influence in Muslim lands could best be achieved by eliminating the regimes that were their mouthpieces in the East. In Zawahiri's terminology, such regimes were set in opposition to the "far enemy," meaning the governments of non-Muslim populations who actually benefited from their dominance of the world order. From a practical perspective, it must have seemed an impossible task to put even a dent into the armor of either of the two superpowers who dominated world politics through the early days of Zawahiri's involvement in the movement. However, his signing of the alliance with bin Lāden that formed the International Islamic Front for Jihad on the Jews and Crusaders in 1998 marked the shift of emphasis from the local to the global picture, and the beginning of his direct confrontation with the United States and its allies.

Zayyāt sees the change in Zawahiri's ideology as a result of his relationship with bin Lāden, whose sites were already set on his enemy across the Atlantic. Zawahiri was in such need of bin Lāden's good connections with the Taliban, and more importantly his financial resources, that he was compelled to adopt his ideological perspectives. This development coincided with a parallel shift in the *jihādi* Islamist movement on the international level. An important source of the new boldness and conviction of the necessity, and now, the possibility, of launching a global jihad against the United States may have been the collapse of the Soviet Union. In the years before the collapse of the Soviet Union, Arab Muslims from all over the Middle East (primarily Egypt, Saudi Arabia, Yemen and Algeria) were moving to Afghanistan to fight the Soviet occupation, and with it, the "Evil Empire" of Soviet atheism. These immigrant fighters, called Arab Afghans, or *mujāhideen* (literally "jihad fighters") were at this time supported by American supplies of weapons and expertise in their struggle against a mutual enemy. Their final victory over the Soviets was to them a victory over domination by modern economies, armies and institutions. Indeed, to the Arab Afghans, the fall of the Soviet Union, which swiftly followed their retreat from Afghanistan, was a direct result of a righteous jihad, fought by a small team of believers against the Soviet Goliath. There is much to suggest that this victory gave the Arab Afghans a taste for the possibility of victory over Western hegemony on the global level.

The Islamist Movement in Egypt

Zayyāt sees the collapse of the Ottoman caliphate and the ensuing Westernization of the Arab world as the main event that marked the beginning of the Islamist movement in Egypt. This is when segments of society began organizing themselves to bring about a return to Islamic traditions and values through the rejection of Western lifestyle and political organization. This goal was originally pursued through *da'wa,* or preaching to other Muslims to live a life guided by religious values.

Zayyāt sees the Islamist movement in Egypt as a response to the colonial experiences of these areas and the continuing tensions caused by Western hegemony in the region. The movement was subjected to the measures taken by Gamāl 'Abdel Nasser, as a component of his modernization program, which began almost immediately after he took power in 1953, to crush Islamist organizations as a presence on the Egyptian political scene. The most prominent of the Islamist organizations at the time was the Muslim Brotherhood. Zayyāt notes that the popularity of these movements increased as faith in Nasser's aspirations dwindled. Specifically, the disappointment caused by the failure of the 1967 Six Day War was a turning point in the popularity of the Islamist movement. The loss resulted in the defeat of the Egyptian forces by Israel and the seizure of the Sinai Peninsula. The Islamist movement offered a different vision that appealed to the disgruntled Egyptian youth.

After Nasser's death in 1970, Anwar al-Sadāt took the reigns of government. He attempted to win the support of religious groups by lightening up restrictions on their political activity. Many more organizations emerged during the Sadāt era with the goal of overthrowing the regime and establishing an Islamic state. The membership and leadership as well as the titles of these organizations developed with the formation of coalitions and splintering along ideological lines. It was also during this period that the movement developed into a call for instituting Islamic *shari'a* as the basis for law and government of the country. Militant action by groups, especially against the Egyptian government, was seen by such groups as a necessary step to replacing the regime with one that would impose an Islamic way of life upon its citizens. Among the first militant groups attempting to change the regime in Egypt was the organization Al-Takfir wal-Hijra, headed by Shukry Mustafa, who held hostage an Egyptian party head in 1977, in an attempt to win the freedom of some imprisoned members.

Today, a few *jihādi* or militant Islamic groups exist in Egypt. The most prominent among them are Islamic Jihad and the Gamā'a al-Islāmiyya, both of which cooperated in the assassination of Sadāt in 1980. The Gamā'a al-Islāmiyya was known as one of the most fierce *jihādi* organizations in Egypt because of the infamous attack on tourists which took place in Luxor in Upper Egypt in 1997. Following that attack, the policies of the group changed radically, leading to the ceasefire agreement of 1999. Although some group members outside of Egypt are believed to have ties with the Al-Qaeda organization, no attacks have been perpetrated by them in Egypt since the agreement to cease attacks against the government. Although Tāha Mūsa (Refā'i Ahmed Tāha), a leading figure in the Gamā'a al-Islāmiyya, appeared in a video in late 2000 with bin Lāden and Zawahiri and vowed to carry out attacks on the United States and Israel, the Gamā'a al-Islāmiyya itself has no official ties with the Al-Qaeda organization. There remains much confusion regarding these groups and their ideologies. As an insider to the movement during the periods he covers, Zayyāt offers an excellent resource for understanding this critical period in the development of the Islamist philosophy that would eventually find its way to Afghanistan and Al-Qaeda.

The book also calls into question the common misconception that religious movements result from poverty and lack of economic opportunities. Zayyāt's detailed description of Egyptian members problematizes this conclusion, reminiscent of the Cold War conception of guerilla movements, by demonstrating that the Islamist movement in Egypt has been driven by well-educated individuals, who had other opportunities that they sacrificed for their cause.

The Al-Qaeda organization

Al-Qaeda (literally "the base") has become the most infamous Islamist organization in the world, due to the many attacks attributed to its members, as well as to outside organizations and groups which have links or sympathies to Al-Qaeda. Some of the attacks that have been attributed to the group include the attack on the American military base in Khobar, Saudi Arabia, the 1995 attack on the Egyptian Embassy in Islamabad, Pakistan, the August 7, 1998 bombing of the US embassies in Kenya and Tanzania, and the infamous attacks on the twin towers in New York City, and on the Pentagon building in Washington, DC.

The Al-Qaeda organization originated in Afghanistan from an earlier organization established to recruit sympathizers from Arab countries to join other "Arab Afghans" by volunteering as *mujāhideen* to fight the secular Soviet presence. It was as a part of this movement, in the 1980s, that Ayman al-Zawahiri and Osāma bin Lāden, heir to millions in Saudi Arabia, joined in what is called by Islamists the Afghan jihad. Ironically, the jihad in Afghanistan was at this time provided with material and logistical support, in the context of Cold War strategy, by the American Central Intelligence Agency.

It was during the fighting against the Soviets in Afghanistan that the relationship between Zawahiri and Bin Lāden was forged. This relationship became official in 1998 upon the signing of an agreement that united Egyptian Islamic Jihad with Al-Qaeda by the formation of the International Islamic Front for Jihad on the Jews and Crusaders. The group aimed to chase out the American presence in the Arabian Gulf, end the embargo against Iraq and seize the holy places in Jerusalem from Israeli control. Many of the details of the organization of Al-Qaeda are as yet mysterious to analysts and experts on the subject. According to Rohan Gunaratna in his book *Inside Al-Qaeda, Global Network of Terror*, the organization consists of political parties, terrorist groups and underground cells which are coordinated and provided with various forms of support through the organization's central leadership in Afghanistan. The degree of organization in the group, and the amount of control that its leadership in Afghanistan has over individual attacks, are still unclear to analysts. For this reason, the inside experience and knowledge contained in the following pages are an important beginning for understanding the root of some of the most pressing obstacles to real security in the contemporary world.

The Road to Al-Qaeda

Introduction
Ayman al-Zawahiri
as I Knew Him

Ibrahim M. Abu-Rabi'

Professor of Islamic Studies and Christian–Muslim Relations,
Hartford Seminary

Of the various accounts of the Islamic movement in contemporary
Egypt, this is the most riveting, insightful, up-to-date, and self-critical.
There are numerous writings on the Islamist movement; however,
few offer an insider's perspective on contemporary Islamism, its trials
and tribulations and the challenges it has faced since the attacks on
the United States on September 11, 2001. In this important work,
Egyptian Islamist lawyer Montasser al-Zayyāt critically discusses the
life, thought, and activities of the founder of the Egyptian Jihad
movement, Dr. Ayman al-Zawahiri, second-in-command of Al-Qaeda,
who has been accused by the United States of being the brains behind
the attacks of September 11. The book offers a detailed analysis of
Zawahiri's social and educational background, religious philosophy,
and involvement with activist Islamist concerns in Egypt before his
permanent departure to Afghanistan in 1987.

   This book is a welcome addition to the meager literature in Western
languages on the role of the Islamist movements in contemporary
politics, their social and economic origins, political and religious
philosophies, and the impact they reputedly have had on world politics,
such as the events surrounding the tragic attacks on the United States
in 2001. An important thesis of this work is that the decision by the
Al-Qaeda leadership in Afghanistan to attack the United States has
created a serious backlash with far-reaching consequences for the

entire world. Undoubtedly, one must understand these ramifications in the post-Cold War context: the military and economic supremacy of the United States in the wake of the Soviet Union's collapse in the early 1990s, the recent decision of the United States to invade Iraq and topple the Ba'thist regime, as well as many other factors. A second thesis of the author is that only a minority of modern Islamist movements have promoted violence against the state in the Muslim world, and that political repression by the governments of the Arab and Muslim worlds have been solely responsible for the creation of such radical movements. Furthermore, the attacks on the United States have given the political elite in the Muslim world more leverage than before to increase their repression of the Islamist movement, and indeed any oppositional voice that dares to call for democracy in these countries. A healthy democratic process is unlikely to take hold in the contemporary Muslim world because of the declared aim of the United States to wage an unlimited battle against terrorism and because of the support the United States has lent in the past to most of the dictatorial regimes in the Muslim world.

At the outset, it is important to underline the fact that Islamism in the modern Arab and Muslim worlds has never been a monolithic phenomenon. There are three types of Islamism in the modern Muslim world: (1) pre-colonial; (2) colonial; and (3) post-colonial. Wahhabism falls into the first category, whereas the Ikhwan of Egypt (the Muslim Brotherhood Movement) falls into the second, and the Jihad and Gamā'a al-Islāmiyya movements fall into the third. By and large, modern Islamism has been the product of modern conditions in the Muslim world, such as the spread of colonialism in the nineteenth and twentieth centuries, the rise of the nation-state, and the failure of the state's modernization programs.

For a number of reasons, modern Arab societies have undergone enormous social, economic, and political changes, which have affected the status of religion and the relationship between religion and society on the one hand, and religion and the state on the other. In the main, these changes have also affected the role and position of the ulama, a class of religious literati who found themselves challenged at the core by the rise of the new nation-state and the Islamic movements.

Although the state in the modern Muslim world has attempted to modernize society using a more or less Westernized approach, it has not been able to shake off the authority of religion. Traditionally, the ulama class legitimized the state with the leverage it had with the masses. Historically, "official Islam" enjoyed the protection and patronage of the ruling elite in Muslim society. Aside from its theological core, Islam grew from an urban environment and is "marked by an urban bourgeoisie outlook."[1] In its formative period and due to Islamic expansion, Islam envisioned a universal community of believers who could transcend ethnic, linguistic and geographic boundaries. However, in spite of the central role of the ulama in providing a universal vision, no corporate "church" body has ever existed in the Muslim world. The ulama, especially in the Sunni world, have more or less stood with the status quo by refusing to support opposition to existing political authority. The mainstream Muslim ulama, providing legitimacy, put their weight behind an Islamic tradition that was pro-status quo and enforced their notion of orthodoxy, often with the support of political authorities. "The Sunni ulama have almost never acted in an organized fashion as if they constituted an institutionally distinct, hierarchically arranged body."[2] In the wake of independence from colonialism, many Muslim countries created Ministries of Religious and Islamic Affairs and encouraged a class of ulama to become official spokespersons of Islam. Very often, the official Islamic discourse shies away from dealing with the immediate issues facing the Arab and Muslim worlds. This discourse fails to deal with such issues as poverty, illiteracy, and oppression within Muslim societies.

Today, this role is being challenged, of course, by the rise of Islamism and its attractive formulation of the religious problematic. Here, the state feels challenged at the core by the rise of resurgence, and in some sense a military confrontation is inevitable, such as that in Syria in the early 1980s and in Algeria in the 1990s. The nationalist state in the 1950s and 1960s seemed to have more than one enemy: both Marxists and Islamists were imprisoned. The post-nationalist and post-1967 Arab state seems to have one enemy: Islamists. Even "at the cultural and ideological planes, the ruling elite imposed the state's ideology on all and barred all free expression, dialogue, and argument."[3] Many an Arab government treats Islamism, including moderate Islamism, "as a security threat," to borrow the words of Egyptian thinker Ahmad Kamal Abu'l Majd.[4] The major Islamist movements in the Arab world were born in the age of imperialism, and the Islamist movements' relationship with the nation-state has been troubled, at best. The absence of democracy in the Arab nation-states has forced a number of small Islamist movements to resort to violence to express and protest the unhealthy conditions of Islamism in the contemporary period.[5]

Since September 11, 2001,[6] the Western world has more or less placed all Islamic movements in one category, that of extremism and terrorism.[7] Some have gone as far as equating Islamism with fascism and totalitarianism and others have considered Islamism to be a threat to the new world order.[8] Few scholars care to study the intellectual and social origins of Islamic resurgence, and even fewer point out that the majority of Islamic movements, although barred from politics, have not resorted to violence against the state. Resurgence has become a refuge for those segments of Arab society that have been alienated by the state and its economic and political policies. The Islamic tradition as a historical and religious depository of ideas and experience has given rise to a new mode of thought, one capable of protecting the alienated and giving them new meaning in a meaningless society.

To understand Islamism, its political nature and possible connection with violence, one must consider the following ideas:[9] (1) far from monolithic, Islamism (or fundamentalism) is a multilayered phenomenon in the Muslim world. It is not a purely religious phenomenon. (2) It is possible to delineate several phases of Islamism: pre-colonial; colonial and post-colonial. (3) Islamism is the product of the major factors affecting the Muslim world in the past two centuries or so. (4) Islamism in large measure is the product of modern European colonialism in the Muslim world and the failure of the modern nation-state to accommodate protest movements in their political systems. (5) The relationship between Islamism and the state in the Muslim world has been complex. In the case of Wahhabism, Islamism and the state have been allied, whereas in other cases, Islamism and the state have been at odds. The state in the modern Muslim world is a nineteenth-century creation prompted by European colonialism. (6) As such,

Islamism has never been a static phenomenon. It has invented a powerful religious discourse to legitimize itself in the eyes of the masses and gain political and economic support. (7) Islamism has been in crisis for the last four decades for many complex reasons: first, because the whole of Muslim tradition has been in crisis and second, because the new guard of Islamism is not satisfied with the achievements or lack thereof on the part of the old guard. This is true in the case of Wahhabism, and bin Lāden is an example.

Islamism has built on a large reservoir of the Sacred – the nebulous Sacred, which has a powerful hold on people's imaginations and allays their fear of death and the afterlife. With economic modernization and the Westernization of certain classes in Arab society, the religious Sacred, instead of becoming less important, has gained new ground. It is not unusual to hear of wealthy dancers and artists who turn to wearing the veil, expressing new forms of religiosity previously unknown in the modern Arab world. The worlds of Westernized art and cinema, notorious bastions of individualism, have given way to the Sacred in the Arab world. Famous singers and artists are gripped by strange dreams that only preachers can interpret. It is the dawn of a new era.

Having said all of this, one must not underestimate the economic base of Islamism in the modern and contemporary Arab world. From its initial construction more or less at the end of the nineteenth century, Islamism was challenged by imperialist economic and political hegemony in the Arab world. In response to imperialism, Islamism sought to construct not just a modernist ethical Islamic order but also an economic one. The rise of the Ikhwan movement in Egypt at the end of the 1920s and in the rest of the Arab world by the end of the 1940s gave the Ikhwan a strong Arab global base that allowed it to compete for the same resources and goals, that is, economic resources and the control of political power. This was true in Syria and Jordan in the 1950s, as it was true in Egypt in the 1940s.

The exile of a substantial number of the Ikhwan's leaders to the Gulf states in the 1960s after the Nasserite repression of the movement in Egypt, and the subsequent migration of hundreds of thousands of Egyptian workers and professionals to the Gulf states in the 1970s and

1980s, gave the Ikhwan new opportunities to construct its financial base in "Arab exile," so to speak. By and large, Islamist groups were banned from competing in the economic field in many Arab countries in the 1980s and 1990s, precisely because of their newly gained power in the Gulf. Many were demonized and pushed to the extreme by the ruling elite in the Arab world. As an economic phenomenon, Islamism has been thinly studied. However, the ban on Islamist politics is at the heart of a ban on Islamist economics as well.

Some Arab thinkers propose a strong connection between the failure of Arab civil society and the emergence of fundamentalism. In other words, they hold the implicit assumption that had conditions in the Arab world been "normal," resurgence would not have emerged so powerfully in the last two decades. It is clear that most opponents of Islamic resurgence object to it on the premise that its main aim is to control the state. Regrettably, only a few serious (and objective) studies exist on religion and its present manifestations in the Arab world. Except for the recent efforts of the Center for Arab Studies in Beirut and a few studies here and there by Arab social scientists and philosophers, a rigorous academic study of religion in the Arab world has been rare. The lack of scholarly studies of religion is evidence of the notion that religion belongs to the incomprehensible domain of the Sacred and the mythical, and does not warrant serious academic treatment except from political and sociological perspectives, or when invoked by the oppressed. This attitude is held by Arab secularists who believe that if religion can be confined to the subjective domain, religious movements will eventually wither away. The position of the state, which is often secular and Western-oriented, is not much different. If the state fails to gain legitimacy through its traditional allies – the ulama – it usually resorts to power as the only solution to political Islam. In other words, the state refuses to treat religion as an evolving reality that is deeply connected with the collective subconscious of the modern Arab people and subject to the ebbs and flows of political, economic and social conditions. Religion becomes instead a simple security threat, one that requires a security response, which means a military, political and intellectual stamping out. This position has been considerably strengthened since the tragic attacks on the United States on September 11, 2001.

Zayyāt's book falls into the genre of religious and political self-criticism. In this sense, it sheds much light on the Islamic movement in the last three decades of the twentieth century. This genre of Islamist writing is somewhat rare; it has captured the imagination of many Islamist leaders since Sayyid Qutb's execution by the Egyptian government in 1966. The strength of the book stems from the fact that its author is one of the most significant members of the Gamā'a al-Islāmiyya, an Islamist organization that at one time advocated violence against the state in Egypt.

Many major developments have taken place in Egypt and the Arab world since Qutb's execution: the imprisonment or exile of thousands of members of the Ikhwan; the 1967 Arab defeat with Israel and the failure of Nasserism to build a new Arab society based on socialism, nationalism, and unity; the death of Nasser in 1970; the accession of Sadāt to power in the same year, and the subsequent de-Nasserization of Egypt in the 1970s and 1980s. These major events, combined with the failure of the state to modernize Egyptian society in the wake of launching its Open Door policy in the early 1970s, created deep social, economic and ideological fissures within Egyptian society, which translated into the rise of several Islamist movements that were inspired by Qutb's confrontational ideology, especially as it developed in his later years in prison before his execution. Zayyāt correctly notes that Qutb, especially in his prison phase, had influenced Zawahiri's thought tremendously and in fact the latter considered Qutb a saint and martyr of the Islamist movement. Qutb's magnum opus *Fi Dhilāl al-Qur'ān* is a document of great importance.[10] According to Zayyāt, the Egyptian regime thought that with Qutb's execution the Islamist movement was dead; little did they realize at the time that the Jihad movement would be born from the womb of Qutbian ideology, and that his execution and radical thought would determine the ideological and religious philosophy of the movement for several decades to come.

Egypt knew a plethora of radical Islamist movements in the 1970s, but none attracted more attention than the Gamā'a al-Islāmiyya and the Jihad movements, which were established in the Egyptian prisons in the 1960s and 1970s. These two movements forged a major alliance that remained more or less intact until 1987. Sadāt's assassination in 1981 put these movements in very difficult positions, since literally thousands of their members were jailed or escaped to countries outside of Egypt.

Zayyāt highlights Zawahiri's social class and educational background. Zawahiri hails from an aristocratic Egyptian family; his grandfather on his mother's side was the late 'Abdel Rahman Azzam Pasha, founder of the Arab League and a major player in Arab and Muslim politics before 1952. Is there a connection between social class and violent Islamism? Zayyāt seems to think that the Islamic faith and ideology exert immense influence on all sorts of people because of the doctrinal message of Islam. In addition to highlighting Zawahiri's social and educational background, Zayyāt persuasively argues that the 1967 Arab defeat by Israel had a tremendous influence on young Zawahiri's thought, as well as that of other Islamists in the 1960s and 1970s. Aside from seeing the Arab military defeat in 1967 in the context of international alliances in the 1950s and 1960s, Western support for Israel, and the "inter-Arab Cold War," to use Malcolm Kerr's favorite term, the defeat was also a reflection of a deeper organizational, social, religious, moral, and linguistic crisis in modern Arab society. Further, it was evidence of a profound lack of familiarity with the "Other" – Israeli society, Zionism, and the threat that a state like Israel would pose to the Arab world and its political and military strategies.[11] If 1948 – the year the state of Israel was established – posed a major shock to Arab and Muslim consciousness, the 1967 defeat, which resulted in the defeat of the "Arab progressive project" of Nasserism and the project of Arab nationalism begun in the nineteenth century, signaled the beginning of a slow and deep awakening of the Arab world to the painful realities, the expansionist project of the Israeli state, and the concrete steps that must be taken in order to strike a balance between this painful reality and Arab potential. For a while, during the most painful days of the defeat, the Arab world showed a strange paralysis of thinking. No one knew what to do. In the words of the Palestinian thinker Ghassan Kanafani, the Arab world was intellectually immobile to the extent that it employed "blind language" in expressing its predicament.[12] The leadership lost its vision and ability to maneuver. Nasser offered his resignation and 'Abd al-Hakim 'Amir committed suicide. All felt a great need to transform Arab society and the Arab person in a real and democratic way.[13] The 1967 defeat proved beyond any shadow of doubt the necessity of establishing new leadership as well as a new Arab individual in a democratic and open atmosphere.

Also, 1967 saw the proliferation of a number of critical Arab writings on the Arab situation. These ranged from the political to philosophical and literary productions. Many contemporary Arab thinkers were forced by the 1967 defeat to reconsider a great number of issues that had been taken for granted, and even question the relevance of the Sacred to Arab thought. The Arab Left and the Islamic and nationalist trends were perturbed by the reasons behind the defeat and sought in their different ways to diagnose and remedy the situation. The Arab intelligentsia was anxious to produce a new intellectual project of self-criticism and rejuvenation. The Arab Left shouldered the responsibility of self-criticism and analysis, and defeat gave the Islamic tendency its best historical moments in decades. In short, a mixture of critical traditions traversed the wounded paths of Arab consciousness. From the Leftist side, Yassin al-Hafiz wrote *Ideology and Defeated-ideology*;[14] Sadiq Jalal al-'Azm wrote *Self-Criticism After Defeat*[15] and *Criticism of Religious Thought*,[16] and Abdallah Laroui wrote *L'idéologie arabe contemporaine*.[17] Islamist thinker Yusuf al-Qaradawi wrote *The Islamic Solution*,[18] and Costantine Zurayk of the nationalist trend wrote *Revisiting the Meaning of Disaster*.[19] These thinkers and others who followed suit posed this question in various ways: "Why have we been defeated and what steps must be taken to remedy the situation?"[20] Zawahiri did not write much about this critical stage in Arab and Muslim history. However, it is important to note that this was the most critical phase in his young life, and perhaps forced him to choose violence against the state as the only way out of the impasse of his society.

Sadāt's assassination in 1981 signaled a major and dangerous shift in the relationship between the state and radical Islamist movements.[21] Upon assuming power, Sadāt was tolerant of these movements because of his insistence on eradicating the power of the left and nationalism in the country, but the state was having a hard time repressing these movements by the end of the 1970s. The state hoped that these movements would fade out due to the severe repression they faced after Sadat's assassination. Zayyāt correctly notes that the Soviet occupation of Afghanistan in 1979 gave a major boost to the Jihad and other radical movements. Zawahiri and thousands of others belonging to radical movements throughout the Muslim world went to Afghanistan to fight the Soviets with an eye toward training a strong cadre of Islamist militants who, upon returning to their countries, would topple the existing regimes. Zayyāt vehemently disagrees with those who argue that Zawahiri was exiled to Afghanistan by order of the Egyptian government. Zawahiri went to Afghanistan for the purpose of implementing his ideas of jihad in a new environment and away from the watchful eyes of the Egyptian secret police. According to Zayyāt, "Afganistan formed the necessary bases for the settlement of Zawahiri and his followers since its environment of jihad and fighting suited very well their desires and objectives."

What is significant about Zayyāt's analysis of the Jihad movement, Al-Qaeda, and the attacks on the United States is that he does not doubt for a second that Al-Qaeda was behind the attacks on the United States. There is a common suspicion in the Arab and Muslims worlds that the September attacks were not the work of Al-Qaeda or any Islamic group but rather were perpetrated by the CIA or Israel. Zayyāt does not seem to buy this argument. He is convinced beyond any shadow of doubt that Zawahiri was the brains behind this attack. In order to prove his point, Zayyāt marshals a great deal of evidence to demonstrate Zawahiri's infatuation with revolutionary or coup d'état conditions, which are predicated on the use of violence to achieve political objectives.

Zayyāt traces Zawahiri's violent approach to politics to the 1980s. In fact, his philosophy of violence had matured long before he went to Afghanistan. Meeting bin Lāden in Afghanistan enabled Zawahiri to recreate his Jihad movement when the two became close friends and strong allies. Zayyāt notes that bin Lāden influenced Zawahiri as much as Zawahiri influenced bin Lāden. Though Zawahiri does not possess bin Lāden's orational or preaching skills, neither does bin Lāden possess Zawahiri's ideological acumen and skill in planning. The two were in agreement over the use of violence against the foreign and domestic enemies of Islam. Coming from aristocratic backgrounds, they shared a common goal: fighting the enemies of Islam. To bin Lāden, American presence in the Gulf was an anathema, and US support for Zionism and Israel was unforgivable. These factors galvanized the "Arab street" behind bin Lāden. Zawahiri influenced bin Lāden in the sense that he was able to sell bin Lāden his "revolutionary *jihadi* ideology," which changed bin Lāden from a *salafi* preacher doing charity work to a *jihādi* fighter immersed in finding legal rulings to fight against the Americans and Zionists. Furthermore, Zawahiri surrounded bin Lāden with some of the most important leaders of the Jihad movement, all of whom highly respected Zawahiri's personality.

The rise of the Taliban movement to power in the early 1990s and its control of most of Afghanistan by 1996 gave an immense political and military boost to Zawahiri's Jihad movement. The Taliban movement came to power on the heels of the failure of the different parties to unite Afghanistan after the Soviet withdrawal. Zayyāt does not tell us much about the reasons behind the rise of the Taliban or why Pakistan provided such enormous assistance. However, he notes that Zawahiri became infatuated with the Taliban philosophy and way of life to the extent that he supported their ban on women's activities outside their homes. In this sense, Zawahiri was more concerned about implementing his revolutionary ideology, controlling power, than in protecting human rights.

The following were probably the reasons for the alliance between the Taliban, on the one hand, and bin Lāden and Zawahiri, on the other: (1) the Taliban's conservative ideology; (2) bin Lāden's financial aid to them; and (3) their role in jihad against the Soviets. The Taliban heavily relied on the Al-Qaeda organization in their dealings with the external world, and it is highly doubtful that they understood the position of Afghanistan in the world political scene after the Soviet withdrawal and the subsequent fall of the Soviet system. In addition to providing a safe haven to members of the Egyptian Jihad movement, the Taliban opened Afghanistan's doors to members of other Islamist organizations (militant or not), such as those of the Gamā'a al-Islāmiyya, who could not return to their original countries for fear of being persecuted by their governments; however, Zayyāt adds that Jihad members enjoyed privileged positions under the Taliban, and were the envy of other organizations.

Because of this privileged position, the Jihad organization began to act as a state within a state in Afghanistan to the extent that Zawahiri planned to assassinate a number of prominent Egyptian political and military leaders, such as the minister of the interior and others. In the 1990s, Egypt was rocked by assassination attempts, made possible by the unlimited amount of money bin Lāden had placed at Zawahiri's disposal. By targeting prominent Egyptian leaders, Zawahiri did not differentiate between domestic and foreign enemies; on the contrary, his priority at this stage (around the mid 1990s) was to wage jihad against those he considered domestic enemies by raising the motto that the way to Jerusalem passes through Cairo, Tunisia, and Algiers. Zayyāt therefore registers his astonishment when in 1996 Zawahiri placed his signature behind the establishment of the International Islamic Front for Jihad on the Jews and Crusaders. Undoubtedly, this change in tactic was forced on Zawahiri after his organization failed to achieve its goals of violent change in Egypt and after the arrest of many of its members in Egypt and overseas.

What is interesting in the last section of the book is Zayyāt's discussion of Zawahiri's criticism of the mainstream Ikhwan, as well as his critique of Zayyāt himself because of the latter's role in advocating peaceful instead of violent means to stop the hemorrhage in Egyptian society.[22] Zawahiri accused Zayyāt of treason to Islam and of being a stooge to the Americans and Israelis. What many ultimately find troublesome about Zawahiri is his propensity for chaotic stands, his use of violence and accusation. According to Zayyāt, Zawahiri's haphazard attitude resulted in his joining the International Front and accounts for his violent bent of mind. In establishing the Front, Zawahiri actually included the Gamā'a al-Islāmiyya without consulting its leaders.

Under the heading "Islamists have paid for the mistakes of Zawahiri," Zayyāt sheds important light on the events surrounding 9/11 and the position of the Islamist movement ever since. He is convinced that the violent attacks on the United States were, first and foremost, the product of an angry, violent, and vengeful mentality that cared less about the consequences of such an attack and more about the immediate damage these attacks would produce and their political ramifications. Because of this carelessness, Zawahiri has placed all Islamic movements, including the mainstream, in grave danger both at home and abroad. Zayyāt does not disagree with either Bin Lāden or Zawahiri that both America and Israel are the main enemies of the Arab and Muslim peoples; however, he does not think that violence can achieve political objectives. The violent attacks on the world's only superpower gave the United States and its allies in the Arab and Muslim worlds the golden opportunity to attack and eradicate all Islamist movements once and for all. Those Islamists who were not members of the Jihad movement and who had sought refuge in Afghanistan because of political oppression in their home countries found themselves face-to-face with America's huge anger and power. They found themselves in a battle that was not of their making and suffered death or imprisonment as a result.

Zayyāt places his fingers on a major problem in the contemporary Arab and Muslim worlds: How to deal with Islamist movements? As a lawyer, Zayyāt does not believe that repression is the solution, and that the 9/11 tragedy has given an upper hand to dictatorial regimes in the Muslim world to practice more oppression against Islamist movements and other oppositional political and religious forces. I believe that one has to embark on a careful examination of the roots of violence in contemporary Arab and Muslim societies. However, Zayyāt does not dwell much on this point. Clearly, the Arab and Muslim worlds have been plagued by tremendous social, economic, and political difficulties that produced violent movements like the Jihad and Gamā'a al-Islāmiyya. The increasing authoritarianism of the political elite and the increasing gaps between the haves and have-nots in the Arab world are not likely to mitigate the problem of violence but will instead permit it to fester. Finally, the unlimited war on terror declared by the Bush administration is not helpful in dealing with the problems either. The American occupation of Iraq is certainly going to enhance the position of extremist Islamist movements in the Muslim world.

This book also raises some serious questions about the United States and radical Islam. It is a well-known story now that the United States began "a serious flirtation with radical Islamist movements,"[23] to use John Cooley's favorite term, immediately after the Soviet invasion of Afghanistan. The international alliance that formed against the Soviets in Afghanistan included the United States, Egypt, Saudi Arabia, Pakistan, and many radical Islamist groups. The war in Afghanistan was, in one sense, the straw that broke the Soviet Union's back, and was what subsequently led to the destruction of the Soviet system and the official end of the Cold War. The capitalist West emerged triumphant in the wake of these momentous world events. Because of this, Afghanistan was left alone to tend to its wounds without any real assistance from key players in the international alliance against the Soviets, except Pakistan and some Islamist groups. It is plausible to argue that in spite of sufficient warning of impending attack on the United States, American authorities did not take them seriously, and most people were caught off guard by their ferocity. In this respect, Cooley has some age-old wisdom to share with the decision makers of the world:

> Perhaps future governments, whether in the United States, the United Kingdom, Russia or less powerful and influential nations, will take to heart this important lesson of late twentieth-century history: When you decide to go to war against your main enemy, take a good, long look at the people behind you whom you chose as your friends, allies or mercenary fighters. *Look well to see whether these allies already have unsheathed their knives – and are pointing them at your own back.*[24]

One must commend Mr. Ahmed Fekry and Sara Nimis of the American University of Cairo for the care and patience with which they have rendered this important book into English. The English library has known many second-rate books written by "objective scholars" on the Islamist movement. This book permits an important voice within contemporary Islamism to represent itself without mediation from the outside.

1

The Aristocrat as Fundamentalist

The first session of the Higher State Security Court that looked into the case known in the press as the "Great Jihad" case was held on December 4, 1982 in a huge hall that was established in the Nasr City Exhibition Center especially to hold the 302 accused Islamists. The hall was full of journalists looking to cover the great event that was shaking Egypt: the assassination of President Anwar al-Sadāt. More importantly, they had all come to see those behind it. Ayman al-Zawahiri and Martyr 'Esām al-Qamari,[1] had just returned from *Sign al Qal'a*, or the Citadel Prison. These two spoke of the torture that members of groups accused of assassinating the late president suffered in prison. Zawahiri held up, as an example of the ongoing torture taking place in the Citadel Prison during the months following the assassination of Sadāt, the case of a young man held in solitary confinement in cell number three of an Egyptian prison often likened to the French Bastille. These prisons were similar, not only in their gloominess, but because of the treatment of political outcasts within their walls. The Citadel Prison, despite its location in the middle of Cairo, somehow alienates those inside from all aspects of normal life. Zawahiri himself had suffered several months of imprisonment within these walls before he was transferred at the beginning of the court proceedings regarding his case. Thus Zawahiri, with the support of 'Esām al-Qamari, called for the transfer of this young man: myself, Montasser al-Zayyāt.

I have always remembered this incident and what Zawahiri did for me despite never having met me. When I met him in the Tora Prison afterwards, I expressed my gratitude for his support, which had relieved much of the pain of the torture and the cruel loneliness that I felt between the walls of the prison. At that time, I felt that my relationship with Zawahiri would witness significant developments, which was indeed the case. Still, I could not have imagined that the same man who had extended to me this anonymous generosity would one day find himself among the most wanted men in the world.

*   *   *

For many years, I found myself probing into his history, looking for incidents that might explain to me and to others hidden sides of his character; I sought events in his past that might disentangle the changes that he underwent. I was searching for the origins of the man whose decisions would eventually shape the new war of the twenty-first century.

Zawahiri was born into an aristocratic family in 1951 in the Cairo suburb of Maadi,[2] which was and still is home to Cairo's most privileged. Zawahiri, who is the product of the renowned Zawahiri and 'Azzām families, was an avid reader. His family noticed his interest in reading, academic excellence and studiousness from a young age. Whenever he got tired of studying, he would not spend time with children his age to play or watch television, but rather read books on religion and Islamic jurisprudence as a pastime. Because of this studious introversion, no group of childhood friends are to be found to tell stories about this time of his life. Still, he was admired by his colleagues, both in school and in his neighborhood in Maadi.

Zawahiri recieved his preparatory and introductory school certificates from the Qawmiyya School. Then he completed his high school certificate in the Maadi School. During his childhood and early youth, he loved literature and poetry, which was rare for a child his age. Although the famous Maadi Sporting Club was so close to his house, he never joined it. He believed that sports, especially boxing and wrestling, were inhumane. For all of these reasons, people who knew him thought he was very tender and softhearted.

In fact, there was nothing weak about the personality of the child Zawahiri. On the contrary, he did not like any opinion to be imposed on him. He was happy to discuss any issue that was difficult for him to understand until it was made clear, but he did not argue for the sake of argument. He always listened politely, without giving anyone the chance to control him.

Despite his strong opinions, he has always been humble, never interested in seizing the limelight of leadership. For instance, although the period when he was studying at Cairo University was a time of great political activity in Egyptian universities, he did not run as a candidate for any of the student union elections throughout his academic career. It was also a period of *da'wa*.[3] Still, Zawahiri did not aspire to be at the center of this religious enthusiasm. Humble as he was, Zawahiri decided not to lead the very *jihādi* movement that he founded in 1987, when he was in Peshawar in Pakistan. At its inception, he gave the leadership of the newly born movement to his friend Sayyid Imām 'Abdel 'Azeez.[4]

Ayman al-Zawahiri was born into a religious Muslim family. Following the example of his family, he not only performed the prayers at the correct times, but did so in the mosque. He used to go to the Hussein Sedqi Mosque, which was close to where he lived. He always made sure that he performed the morning prayers [at sunrise] with a group in the mosque, even during the coldest winters. He attended several classes of Koran interpretation, *fiqh* [Islamic jurisprudence] and Koran recitation at the mosque. Zawahiri always attended a daily lecture delivered by Mostafa Kāmel Wasfi, who was the vice-president of the State Council. Wasfi was also a leading scholar in the science of *Al-Islām al-tanweery* [meaning "enlightened Islam"].

Like his father, he loved reading and seeking knowledge, especially regarding the science of surgery. Like his mother, he observed his prayers, visited the mosque, and read avidly the Koran and other religious books. The books that Zawahiri read and the classes that he took at the mosque did not have a particularly political nature. The books were the same as those that an average Egyptian family might read.

The people who know Zawahiri said that the only relationship he had with a woman was with his wife 'Azza Ahmed Nuwair, who has a degree in philosophy from the Faculty of Arts, Cairo University. They fell in love and got married in 1979 at the Continental Hotel on Opera

Square, which was one of the flashiest hotels at the time. However, it was a conservative Muslim wedding, where there was a hall for men and a separate one for women.

Looking into his aristocratic background, it is impossible to predict that one day he would lead a clandestine movement aimed at toppling the Egyptian regime. Nothing in his youthful good nature suggested that he was to become the second most wanted man in the world. Yet now he is on the run from the United States somewhere in the caves of Afghanistan.

*   *   *

Zawahiri joined the Faculty of Medicine at Cairo University in the academic year 1968–69 and graduated in 1974, with a mark of *gayyid giddan*, the next highest mark possible. He then earned a Masters degree in surgery from Cairo University in 1978 and a PhD in surgery with distinction from a university in Pakistan, while he was living in Peshawar.

When he was arrested on October 23, 1981, it turned out that he had led a clandestine cell before the age of 16. When he was arrested the number of members had reached 13. The authorities discovered that he had led the cell and that he was responsible for the cultural side, which meant that he taught the members the ideological and Islamic framework that they should use in performing *takfir* [the declaration of a regime as infidel]. His criteria for judging political leadership were disseminated undercover between the members. He also coordinated with other *jihādi* groups.[5]

Members of Zawahiri's group

Sayyid Imām 'Abdel 'Azeez, later known as Dr. Fadl or 'Abdel Qader 'Abdel 'Azeez when he moved to Afghanistan, was a close confidant of Zawahiri. He attended a number of decisive meetings with Zawahiri, such as that with 'Abbūd al-Zomor[6] after the assassination of Sadāt on October 6, 1981, a meeting that was designed to convince Zomor to stop any further planned operations. 'Abdel 'Azeez left Egypt in 1985, the same year that Zawahiri left the country. In Peshawar, 'Abdel 'Azeez took over the leadership of the first Islamic Jihad,[7] established in the jihad camps[8] in 1987.

Ameen Yusef al-Domeiry was a pharmacist who participated in financing the cell from the revenues that his pharmacy generated. He also delivered some religious lessons.

The engineer Mohamed 'Abdel Raheem al-Sharqāwi was in charge of recruiting members. He established a turnery workshop in the Gamaliyya district in Cairo to generate profits for the group, as well as using it in manufacturing weapons. The same workshop was used by 'Esām al-Qamari as a hideaway after he escaped from the Army in 1981.

Khāled Medhat al-Fiqi used his flat in Maadi as a warehouse for the group's weapons and ammunition. In 1988, he was accused of helping 'Esām al-Qamari, Khāmis Muslim and Mohamed al-Aswāni escape from the Tora Prison. He was also accused in 1999, along with Zawahiri's brother Mohamed al-Zawahiri, of planning *jihādi* operations in Egypt.

Khāled 'Abdel Samee' was arrested while walking along the Nile in Maadi immediately after Sadāt was assassinated. In his possession, the authorities found a bag full of bombs, which was the first in the string of clues that eventually led them to Zawahiri.

Mohamed al-Zawahiri is a civil engineer, who was pushed by his brother Ayman to leave Egypt in 1981 to find financial resources for the cell. That year, when Sadāt was assassinated, he was abroad working in a Gulf country. He was accused in absentia, but was later acquitted. In 1998, he was accused again in absentia in the case known in the media as the "Returnees from Albania" case,[9] which I discuss on a number of occasions in this book. He was later sentenced to death and some press reports said the United Arab Emirates handed him over to Egypt in 2000, but the Egyptian authorities did not comment on this information, which has not been verified from an unbiased source.

'Esām al-Qamari was an officer in the Egyptian Armed Forces. He was the link between Zawahiri and another cell inside the Army. His role is discussed at greater length later in the book. Other members included Yusef 'Abdel Mageed, 'Esām Hendāwi, Mostafa Kāmel

Mostafa, 'Abdel Hādi al-Tunsi and Nabeel al-Bora'i, who was the owner of a bookshop in Maadi.

Jihādi groups before the assassination of Sadāt

The period that preceded the assassination of Sadāt in 1981 witnessed a rapid growth in *jihādi* groups. Multiple factions were divided on which approaches were most ethical and which most effective in bringing about change. *Al-Ikhwan al-Muslimeen* or the Muslim Brotherhood[10] succeeded in 1979 in recruiting active students in Lower Egypt,[11] notable among whom were Dr. 'Abdel Moni'm Abu al-Fotūh, Dr. 'Esām al-'Eriyān and Dr. Ibrahim al-Za'farāni. Several other groups besides Zawahiri's, described above, were functioning in this period:

The Gamā'a al-Islāmiyya [literally "Islamic Group"] was a *jihādi* organization made up of university students, especially from Upper Egyptian[12] universities such as Menya, Beni Suef, Suhaj, Assyūt, Qena, Aswan, as well as some faculties of Cairo University. The group was led by Karam Zohdi and included other well-known figures such as Osāma Hāfez, Salāh Hāshim, Tal'at Fou'ād Qāssem, Nāgeh Ibrahim, 'Esām Derbālah, Refā'i Tāha and Hamdi 'Abdel Rahmān. Two Upper Egyptian leaders well known among Islamists in that region broke this Upper Egyptian unity by joining the Muslim Brotherhood, namely Mohiyee al-Deen 'Eisa and Abu al-'Ela Mādi.

Mohamed 'Abdel Salām Farag's group was popular in Boulaq, Nahia and Kerdasa,[13] the area where its founder and namesake lived. Farag himself was married to the sister of two of the most prominent Islamic Jihad figures, namely Yehia and Magdi Ghareeb Fayād. The Zomor family had a lot of power in the village of Nahia, one of the areas where Farag's group was popular. Both 'Abbūd and Tāriq al-Zomor lived there. Other parts of the Zomor family were based in Cairo suburbs such as 'Ein Shams, where Nabeel al-Maghrebi, Hussein 'Abbās and 'Abdel Hameed 'Abdel Salam lived, as well as in Lower Egypt governorates such as Beheira, where 'Ata Tāyel Hameeda Raheel lived.[14]

Mohamed Sālem al-Rahāl was a Palestinian–Jordanian studying at Al-Azhar University.[15] He founded his own group, as well as having a prominent role in bringing together other *jihādi* groups. When the authorities found out about his activities, he was arrested and eventually deported in May, 1980. Sālem al-Rahāl was a close friend of mine. He used to visit me in my residence on Dobreih Street in Cairo, but we would also meet in other parts of the city. The last time I was supposed to meet him was in a mosque in Shubra[16] in 1980. I went there at the designated time but he did not show up. I later learned that he had been deported. Kamāl al-Sayyid Habeeb later replaced him in leading the group.

The assassination of Sadāt

In 1979, Mohamed 'Abdel Salām Farag managed to unite several small *jihādi* groups under his leadership. In 1980, he made an agreement with Karam Zohdi, the leader of the Gamā'a al-Islāmiyya, to unite all of these *jihādi* groups with the Gamā'a al-Islāmiyya. The group resulting from this merger was led by Sheikh 'Omar 'Abdel Rahmān, a professor at the Faculty of *Osoul al-Deen* [meaning "Fundamentals of Islam"] at the Assyūt branch of Al-Azhar University. This coalition led directly to the assassination of Sadāt on October 6, 1981, the same day that the Armed Forces were celebrating the October War victory.[17] Following the assassination, a battle began in the governorate of Assyūt[18] between the Gamā'a al-Islāmiyya and the government authorities. This ended in the arrest of most of the members of the two groups. The authorities divided them into three categories.

The first category of detainees included those who actually implemented the assassination during the military parade. These were led by Khāled al-Islāmboli, 'Abdel Hameed 'Abdel Salām, 'Ata Tāyel Hameeda Raheel and Hussein 'Abbās. The list of accused members also included Mohamed 'Abdel Salām Farag who planned the operation, as well as Sheikh 'Omar 'Abdel Rahmān and the rest of the members who knew of the assassination before it happened, and participated in it one way or another. The number of accused members in this category reached 24. They were tried for assassination, accessory to assassination, and incitement, before the military court[19] presided over by Sameer Fādel. The court sentenced the first five members to death, while the rest of the accused were sentenced to life imprisonment. The court, however, acquitted Sheikh 'Omar 'Abdel Rahmān, and Sayyid al-Salamūni, a professor at the Faculty of Education, 'Ein Shams University.

The fate of the second group of detainees was referred to the Higher State Security Court[20] in what was called the Jihad case. The accused included 302 group members, led by Sheikh 'Omar 'Abdel Rahmān, who is currently sentenced to life imprisonment in an American prison. The list of accused members included 'Abbūd al-Zomor, an officer in the Military Intelligence. The most prominent leaders of this group from Upper Egypt were Karam Zohdi, Nāgeh Ibrahim, Fou'ād al-Dawālibi, Osāma Hāfez, Tal'at Fou'ād Qāssem, Refā'i Tāha, 'Ali al-Sherif and Hamdi 'Abdel Rahmān. Leaders from Cairo and Lower Egypt included Ayman al-Zawahiri, Sayyid Imām 'Abdel 'Azeez, Tharwat Salāh Shehāta, Nabeel Na'eem 'Abdel Fatah, Ayman al-Domeiri, Kamāl al-Sayyid Habeeb and Refā'i Sorūr. Other members were tried for leadership of the group that broke into the Security Administration Building in Assyūt and the robbery of a number of jewelry shops in Naga' Hammādy and Shubra al-Kheima on the morning of October 8, 1981, a couple of days after the assassination of Sadāt.

None of this group was sentenced to death, but the prominent accused members were sentenced to harsh imprisonment, while the great majority were sentenced to three years in prison. These included Zawahiri, who was convicted of possession of a firearm. The remaining 170 accused members in this second category were acquitted. These comparatively light sentences given to those standing trial in the Jihad case revealed that the regime had decided to try to cool the tension between themselves and *jihādi* activists.

It was in this context that the third group would be tried. This group was made up of 178 members who were accused of subscribing to the *jihādi* ideology. At this time, I was at the top of the list of accused members. The list also included prominent figures from the Gamā'a al-Islāmiyya such as Mohamed Shawqi al-Islāmboli and 'Abdel Akher

Hammād, as well as prominent *jihādi* figures such as Magdi Sālem and ʿAdil ʿAbdel Mageed.

The trial lasted for about two years, resulting in the decision of the Higher State Security Court to postpone looking into our case indefinitely. This led to the release of all members; the case was never brought up again. In retrospect, this was a message from the regime that they wanted to cool tensions with *jihādi* groups. At the time, we did not decipher it clearly, and we missed what could have been a key opportunity. It was the first of many that we would see pass us by.

Zawahiri, like many young people, was shaken by the trauma of the defeat in June 1967,[21] a defeat that led to the collapse of many idols that had haunted the public for many years. This was expressed in his book *Fursān Taht Raye tal-Nabby*, meaning *Knights Under the Banner of the Prophet*, especially when he wrote:

> The unfolding of events impacted the course of the *jihādi* movements in Egypt, namely, the 1967 defeat and the ensuing symbolic collapse of Gamāl ʿAbdel Nasser,[22] who was portrayed to the public by his followers as the everlasting invincible symbol. The *jihādi* movements realized that woodworms had eaten at this icon, and that it had become fragile. The 1967 defeat shook the earth under this idol until it fell on its face, causing a severe shock to its disciples, and frightening its subjects. The *jihādi* movements grew stronger and stronger as they realized that their avowed enemy was little more than a statue to be worshiped, constructed through propaganda, and through the oppression of unarmed innocents. The direct influence of the 1967 defeat was that a large number of people, especially youths, returned to their original identity: that of members of an Islamic civilization. This return came only after two decades of following in the footsteps of the Kremlin, and before that of the West, in the form of the British High Commissioner.

> Islamic awakening started as a spontaneous result and became rampant in numerous segments of Egyptian society, especially in the universities. Numerous groups turned to Islamic *daʿwa* in an attempt to revive Islamic activity after a long absence, and to stand up to the dark forces of communism that controlled all official

circles. Within the universities there were religious groups that tried to propagate the true teachings of Islam and its pure principles. Muslim preachers from this group had access to droves of university students that gravitated towards Islam and its causes.

The leaders of the Islamic student movement included Dr. 'Abdel Mon'im Abu al-Fotūh and Dr. 'Esām al-'Eriyān in Cairo, Dr. Ibrahim al-Za'farāni in Alexandria, as well as Karam Zohdi, Nāgeh Ibrahim, Abu al-'Ela Mādi, Refā'i Tāha, Mohamed Shawqi al-Islāmboli, Osāma Hāfez, Salāh Hāshim, and Ahmed al-Zayyāt in Upper Egypt. Influenced by a number of writers, Zawahiri chose the path of clandestine activity.

Writers and figures who influenced Zawahiri's ideology

The martyr Sayyid Qutb was one of the most important figures in terms of his impact on Zawahiri. Qutb's writing was important in shaping Zawahiri's principles. His book *Fi Dhilāl al-Qur'ān* [meaning *Under the Umbrella of the Koran*] formed the framework for Zawahiri's ideology and his approach to effecting change. The book is an interpretation of the Holy Koran based on ideas that dawned on Qutb when he was serving a prison sentence for false charges brought against him by Gamāl 'Abdel Nasser. Zawahiri's love for Qutb is clear in that he quotes him in almost everything he publishes.

In his book *Knights Under the Banner of the Prophet*, Zawahiri wrote:

Sayyid Qutb underscored the importance of monotheism in Islam, and that the battle between it and its enemies is at its core an ideological difference over the issue of the oneness of God. It is the issue of who has the power: God and his *shari'a* [literally the Islamic "path," refers to the guidelines by which good Muslims should live] or man-made, materialistic laws.

Zawahiri expresses his admiration for Qutb, saying:

Although the Qutb group was oppressed and tortured by Nasser's regime, the group's influence on young Muslims was paramount.

Qutb's message was and still is to believe in the oneness of God and the supremacy of the divine path. This message fanned the fire of Islamic revolution against the enemies of Islam at home and abroad. The chapters of this revolution are renewing one day after another.

In Zawahiri's eyes, Sayyid Qutb's words struck young Muslims more deeply than those of his contemporaries because his words eventually led to his execution. Thus, those words both provided the blueprint for his long and glorious lifetime, and eventually led to its end. The Nasserite regime thought that it had administered a fatal blow to the Islamist movement by executing Qutb and his companions, and detaining thousands of the followers of the movement. In fact, the stillness of the surface hid what was beneath: a boiling reaction to Qutb's philosophy. His teachings gave rise to the formation of the nucleus of the contemporary *jihādi* movements in Egypt.

Another important influence on the thinking of Zawahiri was Sāleh Seriya. Seriya arrived in Egypt after Sadāt's decision to release the leaders of the Muslim Brotherhood group. Upon his arrival, he contacted prominent figures in the Muslim Brotherhood such as Zeinab al-Ghazāli and Hassan al-Hodeibi. He managed to form groups of youths and urged them to stand up to the ruling regime.

Zawahiri describes Seriya as

a well-spoken, well-read and cultured man. He completed his PhD in education at 'Ein Shams University. He was well versed in a number of Islamic disciplines. I saw Seriya only once, at an Islamic camp[23] organized in the Faculty of Medicine, in which he was invited to deliver a speech. As soon as I listened to the speech, I was moved by his words, which I thought had a very strong message for upholding Islam. I decided that I should meet him but all my attempts were in vain.

In his writings, Zawahiri also mentions the Technical Military Academy coup d'état, which was the first coup against Sadāt and was led by Seriya. The coup did not succeed. Zawahiri explained the failure as primarily due to poor training of the young men who attacked the guards of the Academy gates. Overall, coup leaders did not consider the realities of the situation. The lesson taken from the failure of this operation was that those who were performing jihad failed to draw a distinction between the Soviet-style Nasserite era and the new Sadāt era. They simply saw both of them as enemies. Although the operation was foiled at its beginning, it marked a significant change in the course of the Islamist movements: they had decided to take arms against the government.

Yehia Hāshim was both a great influence on Zawahiri, and a friend to him. In a description of Hāshim, Zawahiri writes:

> He is a vanguard of the *jihādi* movements in Egypt, and deservedly so as God has granted him great attributes, namely his noble spirit and strong determination. These have led him to sacrifice all that he has, oblivious to the worldly matters for which others compete.

Indeed, Yehia Hāshim held the highly sought position of district attorney. Although this is a position to which many youths aspire, his success never led to arrogance, and he was always ready to sacrifice himself for God.

Zawahiri met Hāshim in the wake of the 1967 defeat. Hāshim joined Zawahiri's group but did not stay with them for long, preferring to strengthen his links with the Muslim Brotherhood. Later, Hāshim himself became even more convinced of the *jihādi* emphasis on armed struggle and strengthened his ties with Sāleh Seriya's group. Hāshim eventually left to hide in the mountains of Menya[24] to prepare for armed struggle through guerilla warfare, but the Egyptian authorities broke into his refuge, where he fought them and was martyred.

'Esām al-Qamari is a contemporary of Zawahiri, and they had much in common. Both men found meaning in Islamism when they were in high school. It was an identity that they both discovered was fundamental to themselves, but which had been dormant in both. They shared the belief that Islamism was essential for the good of the entire *umma* [the Islamic nation or community of believers, the greater nation of all Muslims]. Zawahiri never hid his admiration for Qamari, who joined the Military Academy because of a deeply held belief in the necessity of change, which they decided could only be achieved through a coup. Zawahiri and Qamari agreed that a coup was the best way to replace what they considered secular governments, and establish an Islamic government that institutes Islamic *shari'a*. They believed that a coup would be the fastest way to jump to power with minimum losses and bloodshed in their struggle against the regime.

While I was in prison, I noticed that Qamari was very strong. He controlled the *jihādi* elements, including Zawahiri himself. I witnessed this during the struggle that took place between the members of the Gamā'a al-Islāmiyya and the many splinter *jihādi* elements in the Tora Prison over whether Sheikh 'Omar 'Abdel Rahmān was capable of leadership of the group despite his blindness.[25] Qamari's voice was the loudest, wholeheartedly opposing 'Abdel Rahmān's leadership on account of his poor eyesight. This issue led eventually to the demise of the coalition between the various *jihādi* groups under the leadership of Farag and the Gamā'a al-Islāmiyya. Qamari was a courageous man who did not fear anyone in his struggle to follow the path of God, even to the extent of rashness. It was the rashness which caused him a lot of problems with his brethren from the Islamist movements in prison, especially regarding the debate over 'Abdel Rahmān's leadership of the newly unified Islamic group.

I personally had a lot of respect for 'Esām al-Qamari. Whenever I met Qamari, he showed great affection towards me and I reciprocated this feeling, which turned some people against me at the time. Still, he had delegated Zawahiri to represent him to the press and the court in the second session of the Jihad case, having not attended the first. As his representative, Zawahiri spoke of the inhumane treatment inside the Citadel Prison, and of my case in particular. It was that plea which forced the authorities to transfer me, along with my fellow Islamic activists, to regular prisons.

Sayyid Imām 'Abdel 'Azeez was also significant, although many overlooked the great influence that he had on Zawahiri, knowing only that Zawahiri recruited him to join the old group before the events of 1981. A closer look at their relationship reveals that 'Abdel 'Azeez deeply influenced the way Zawahiri thinks. The very length of their good relationship – from the 1960s until the second half of the 1990s

– suggests its importance. Zawahiri prioritized 'Abdel 'Azeez over himself by choosing him to be the first leader of Islamic Jihad, the group which Zawahiri established in Peshawar in Pakistan. 'Abdel 'Azeez remained at the helm of Islamic Jihad until 1992, when Zawahiri took over leadership of the group following a disagreement between the two regarding an issue of jurisprudence. During his leadership of Islamic Jihad, 'Abdel 'Azeez remained in charge of the *Shari'a* Committee in the group. He wrote its constitution, known as *Al-'Omda fi E'dād al-'Odda* [*The Basis for Preparedness*]. The book includes the group's ideology, its objectives and the means it uses to achieve them, among other issues. For example, it states that it is *harām* [meaning "forbidden" by Islamic *shari'a*] to go inside the Parliament building or to run for elections. Many people thought wrongly that *The Basis for Preparedness* was written by Zawahiri. This is false, although Zawahiri did write another book entitled *Al-Gami' fi Talab al-'Elm al-Shar'i* [*The Comprehensive Guide to Seeking Noble Knowledge*] that contributed enormously to the formation of the group's ideology. This book created some tensions between them, which eventually led to 'Abdel 'Azeez abandoning the group.

Osāma bin Lāden also had an appreciable impact on Zawahiri, although the conventional wisdom holds the opposite to be the case. Both are true to a certain degree. Bin Lāden's impact on Zawahiri is examined in greater detail in later chapters.

2

The Aftermath of Sadāt's Assassination

During the three stages of the trial following the assassination of Anwar al-Sadāt, the Egyptian authorities distributed us amongst different prisons, where we spent more than two years. I used to go to the Tora Prison every now and then, although I was placed in the Abu Za'bal Prison. That is where I met Ayman al-Zawahiri.

It was there that I witnessed the debates regarding whether Dr. 'Omar 'Abdel Rahmān should lead the newly born coalition between the various *jihādi* groups and the Gamā'a al-Islāmiyya. This was the most violent crisis facing all the *jihādi* activists spread among the city's prisons.

This crisis was exacerbated by the general feeling of failure, which had overcome the new group after the disappointing result of several rushed and ill-conceived operations. These operations took place between September 5, 1981, when Sadāt decided to confine 1,536 political activists, including a large number from Islamist movements, and the October 6, 1981 assassination of Sadāt during a military parade in Nasr City.[1] Many heated discussions raged in prison over the causes of these failures. Some members were accused of negligence and of not having completed the tasks with which they had been entrusted. For instance, the expansion of the operation to break into the Assyūt Security Administration Building on October 8, 1981, which coincided with the *'eid al-adha* [The Feast of the Sacrifice], left more than 100 people dead. The high death toll served as a clue to the Egyptian authorities that the threat lay not only in the small group that implemented the assassination, but in their supporters who were clearly in the hundreds.

A number of leading figures in the *jihādi* movement argued against the nomination of Sheikh 'Omar 'Abdel Rahmān as the leader of the new coalition on account of his lack of eyesight. One of the strongest opponents of 'Abdel Rahmān's leadership was the martyr 'Esām al-Qamari, followed by Zawahiri, among others.

It is amazing that Refā'i Tāha, leader of the Gamā'a al-Islāmiyya, maintained such good relations with Zawahiri after their deep differences in prison. Refā'i Tāha took over the leadership of the Gamā'a al-Islāmiyya at a very critical time following his release and travel to Afghanistan, until he was forced to resign because of the Luxor Massacre in November 1997.[2] I recall that their relationship reached its lowest ebb when they were in prison in 1983. I still remember Tāha's words to me: he said that Zawahiri was fanning the fire of dissension by encouraging 'Esām al-Qamari to argue against 'Abdel Rahmān's leadership.

When I met Zawahiri in the cell of the Tora Prison Hospital, he answered my questions very quietly, maintaining that what Tāha said was groundless, and that he held deep respect for 'Abdel Rahmān. He agreed that 'Abdel Rahmān had sacrificed much, including his social and academic status. However Zawahiri pointed out that 'Abdel Rahmān would be wise to end this serious division within the group by giving up the leadership, just as 'Ali Ibn Abi Tālib, the Prophet Mohamed's cousin, gave up the caliphate to Mu'awiya to avoid bloodshed. In the end 'Abdel Rahmān persisted in his bid for leadership, and the difference eventually led to the break-up of the coalition between the *jihādi* groups and the Gamā'a al-Islāmiyya.

When stories of abuses in the prisons surfaced, Justice 'Abdel Ghaffār Mohamed Ahmed called for the investigation of the officers accused of performing the torture. Zawahiri was not interested in filing a court case against the authorities for the abuses he suffered during the Jihad case. When investigations were eventually conducted by the Public Prosecution Office, he contented himself with testifying as a witness to the torture of other members.

I met with Zawahiri after he was released from the Jihad case. Soon thereafter, in 1985, he traveled to Jeddah, Saudi Arabia, where he was planning to work for a hospital. Only upon visiting him there did I learn what had prompted him to leave Egypt for Saudi Arabia.

I was able to visit him in Saudi Arabia when traveling there to perform *'omra* [the minor pilgrimage]with Magdi Sālem, a prominent figure in Islamic Jihad who is now serving 20 years in prison for his involvement in the case of the *Talāe' al-Fateh* [literally the "Vanguards of Conquest"].[3] I visited him in the Ibn al-Nāfees hospital, where he was working in Jeddah. He looked very sorrowful. The scars left on his body from the indescribable torture he suffered caused him no more pain, but his heart still ached from it.

The torture he suffered was not proportionate to his comparatively minor role in the assassination of Sadāt. The authorities were particularly harsh with him not because of his deeds, but because of his connections. They discovered after arresting him that he was in contact with a number of officers from the Egyptian Armed Forces. These included the martyr 'Esām al-Qamari, an Armed Forces officer. Qamari fled from the army when, in March 1981, the authorities discovered his Islamist orientations. Zawahiri was also incriminated by his links with Captain 'Abdel 'Azeez al-Gamāl and First Lieutenant 'Awni 'Abdel Mageed. I met Gamāl and 'Abdel Mageed only after the incident, during the proceedings of the Jihad case.

Despite all that he had suffered physically, what was really painful to Zawahiri was that, under the pain of torture, he was forced to testify against his fellow members in the case against 'Esām al-Qamari and other officers. Zawahiri was taken from the Tora Prison to the Higher Military Court to give testimony against other *jihādi* members from the army. Under these conditions, he admitted that they formed a movement inside the army to topple the regime and institute an Islamic government.

After he was arrested on October 15, 1981, Zawahiri informed the authorities of Qamari's whereabouts. He had taken refuge in a small mosque where he used to pray and meet Zawahiri and other members of the group. It was this painful memory which was at the root of Zawahiri's suffering, and which prompted him to leave Egypt for

The Aftermath of Sadāt's Assassination   **31**

Saudi Arabia. He stayed there until he left for Afghanistan in 1987. During the three years following his arrival in Afghanistan, his leadership among *jihādi* Islamists became more prominent, as he worked to regroup the disorientated group members.

Intelligence officer 'Abbūd al-Zomor, who remained in the Tora Prison until 1987, was the most well-known symbol of the *jihādi* movement. He was the incarcerated leader, and the attention of all jihad supporters hung on his messages, recommendations and literature. While Zomor was enjoying this great popularity, Magdi Sālem was his representative outside of the prison and the acting leader of the *jihādi* movement. Sālem was also supported by the Palestinian–Jordanian 'Esām Mateer. It had become the most popular Islamist movement at the time and was most successful in recruiting young members.

As it turned out, events did not develop in line with Zomor's plans. Instead, they followed the direction of Zawahiri's aspirations and ambitions. Sālem worked in a trading business, which required him to travel abroad regularly. His frequent absence eventually led to the loosening of his grip on *jihādi* activists in Egypt. Mateer's activeness had made up for Magdi Sālem's absence until the former was arrested by the authorities and deported to Jordan. Mateer's departure left a huge vacuum amongst Zomor's supporters.

The Gamā'a al-Islāmiyya

Meanwhile, the leading member of the Gamā'a al-Islāmiyya, Mohamed Shawqi al-Islāmboli, moved from the city of Malawy in Menya to set up a commercial project in Cairo. He opened a bookshop in 'Ein Shams,[4] near the areas that the Gamā'a al-Islāmiyya controlled. A number of Gamā'a al-Islāmiyya members lived in 'Ein Shams, including 'Abdel Hameed 'Abdel Salām, Hussein 'Abbās, and Nabeel al-Maghrebi. It is noteworthy that while Khāled al-Islāmboli was a member of Islamic Jihad, his brother Mohamed Shawqi al-Islāmboli was a member of the Gamā'a al-Islāmiyya. Mohamed Shawqi al-Islāmboli owned a bookshop which sold religious books and tapes of religious sermons. The shop doubled as a center for his activities, namely, promoting the sermons delivered in the mosque by Sheikh

'Omar 'Abdel Rahmān after the leader's release from prison in 1984. He also promoted recordings of Sheikh 'Abdel Rahmān's Koranic recitation, a skill for which the Al-Azhar professor was well known. Thus, Mohamed al-Islāmboli's bookshop, located on the ground floor of the Sa'b Ibn Sāleh Mosque, became the first headquarters of the Gamā'a al-Islāmiyya in Cairo. Mohamed al-Islāmboli's charisma and the support of his family provided the main force behind the growing popularity of the group in Cairo. The mother of the Islāmboli brothers was a component of this force, serving as a symbol of perseverance after the loss of her son Khāled to the cause. Subsequently, the Gamā'a al-Islāmiyya started entering Lower Egypt, where it did not have any presence before the assassination of Sadāt in October 1981.

Regrouping from abroad

In some ways, Zawahiri's mission of regrouping the *jihādi* movement in Egypt from Afghanistan was easier than the task facing the leadership of the Gamā'a al-Islāmiyya. Many young people traveled to Afghanistan to take part in fighting the Soviets and freeing Kabul from communist occupation. Zawahiri, whose relationship with Osāma bin Lāden was very good, could offer a good reception to young travelers arriving in the camps that bin Lāden had established. There he offered them military training and mental and political preparation for their battle. This atmosphere facilitated Zawahiri's efforts to tighten control over newcomers and recruit them into his new movement which he hopes will achieve the aim that he has worked toward all his life: toppling the regime in Egypt. Zawahiri clearly saw this as an objective, from the first day he joined a clandestine cell in 1968. I say this not to defame Zawahiri, but to give an accurate historical representation of his approach.

For this reason, as he continued his efforts in Afghanistan, Zawahiri maintained links in Cairo. His supporters in the capital city recruited the remaining members of Zomor's group and helped them travel to Afghanistan. Nabeel Na'eem 'Abdel Fatah and Tharwat Salāh Shehāta promoted Zawahiri's writings and ideas. These became popular, and enabled Zawahiri to recruit almost all of the members of Zomor's group.

Zawahiri's yellow-covered booklets found their way into the hands of many Cairo youths. The booklets were distributed secretly, but the enormous popularity that 'Abdel Fatah and Shehāta worked to win for them eventually caught the attention of the authorities. They sensed the danger the two men posed in disseminating *jihādi* beliefs, and arrested 'Abdel Fatah in 1991. Still, Shehāta managed to escape arrest by traveling to Afghanistan on a counterfeit passport. There he became the second most important man in Zawahiri's movement.

When I met Zawahiri in Jeddah, before he established his movement, he told me that one of the reasons for the failure of the Gamā'a al-Islāmiyya is that it was so concerned about secrecy that it would never distribute any literature that appealed to the people. He explained that it was for this reason that clandestine movements do not work in Egypt. He added that any Islamic movement that does not connect with the masses loses any reason to exist. This was the impetus for his production of literature articulating and promoting his ideology.

Zawahiri's vision

Before analyzing this ideology, a discussion of his charisma is in order. Zawahiri is very good-natured, tender and quiet. He talks so little that he could almost be called introverted. His ideas are always organized, so when he speaks, he expresses himself very well. He is very cool-headed. He does not get angry easily, which is why he is capable of making critical decisions at difficult times.

In order to understand Zawahiri's ideology, his social background must be analyzed at a level deeper than his aristocratic roots. His family has an old revolutionary heritage. His paternal grandfather is Mohamed al-Zawahiri, a renowned *azhari*[5] scholar who resisted occupation and the corruption of the royal family. His maternal grandfather is 'Abdel Rahmān Pasha 'Azzām, the first secretary general of the Arab League (or League of Arab States), who sincerely tried to unify the Arabs. His maternal uncles include Sālem 'Azzām, who runs the European Islamic Council in London and Mahfūz 'Azzām, vice president of the opposition Egyptian Labor Party. In his interrogations in 1981, Zawahiri stated that his uncle Sālem provided him with money, and Mahfūz is believed to have previously had links with the Muslim Brotherhood. Later Zawahiri testified that these confessions were extracted from him under torture and that 'Azzām did not give him any money. This testimony led to the acquittal of the 'Azzām brothers. In sum, Zawahiri's family comes from a revolutionary heritage, implanting in him the belief in revolt against bad circumstances. This may explain why, following the June 1967 defeat by Israel, Zawahiri decided to give up his aristocratic lifestyle for his cause.

The aristocratic background of Zawahiri and of his ally Sheikh Osāma bin Lāden reveals that the claim that the appearance of armed Islamic groups is the result of economic and social factors is groundless. Many of the accused members in several cases were from high social classes, including businessmen and professionals, who got arrested and tried due to their Islamic beliefs.

When someone believes in an idea, especially if this idea is related to a noble and ancient civilization like Islam, this belief can transcend social and class considerations. Poverty may indeed lead to violence, but it is not poverty which leads to the Islamic ideology. The followers of Islamic thought include both the rich and the underprivileged. Just as the underprivileged turn to Islamic institutions as a source of social solidarity and justice against their plight, the privileged look to Islamic institutions as a way of getting closer to God, who gave them this money, by putting it towards the needy.

Whether or not I agree with Zawahiri, I respect him as one who could have used his social background to make social and financial gains for himself, but chose instead to sacrifice this potential for his ideals and beliefs. Even having made such noble sacrifices, he is still humble and self-effacing, which is part of the reason for the dedication and love that his followers feel for him.

Unlike the family of Osāma bin Lāden, who disowned him and issued a press statement to the world announcing as much, Zawahiri's family has not disowned him, even at the worst of times. They have resisted all pressures to forsake him, and respect the ideology he adopts. In their efforts to consider him still one of them, Zawahiri's family has tried to find excuses for him, and for his behavior. Some members of his family speculate as to the reasons for his departure from Egypt, the adoption of an armed approach to the struggle against the government, along with other developments in his life. They see his flight as an escape from the threat of torture by the Egyptian regime. I see this conclusion as belittling to Zawahiri and his beliefs, with all due respect to his family.

Unlike them, I see Zawahiri as an important public figure whose effect on the course of events in Egypt suggests the need for a closer look at his thoughts, approach and mechanisms. For any who might have doubted this, the unfolding of events that followed his alliance with Osāma bin Lāden in February 1998 underline the need for such careful analysis. These events include the bombing of the American embassies in Nairobi and Darussalam,[6] the bombing of the American destroyer *Cole* in the Aden Port in Yemen[7] and the first court verdict issued against him by a military court in Egypt in the case known in the press as the Returnees from Albania case, in which he was sentenced to death in absentia.

Then the world witnessed the bloody incidents of September 11, 2001, when explosions in New York and Washington, DC killed thousands. The American authorities announced that the parties responsible were both Osāma bin Lāden and Ayman al-Zawahiri, making them the first and second most wanted men respectively by the Americans. This event proved that Zawahiri's ideological state has reached its apex.

I begin looking into Zawahiri's ideology by analyzing his own words in the form of both confessions during the interrogations of the Jihad case of 1981, in addition to his own writings.

Zawahiri's confessions
Case No. 462 of 1981, Higher State Security Court
(the Jihad case)

In response to a question by Higher State Security district attorney Mahmūd Mas'ūd on November 2, 1981, Zawahiri made the following statement:

I want to say that in 1966 and 1967 I was a member of a religious cell headed by Isma'eel Tantāwi and there was another member called Sayyid Hanafi. Our objective was to topple the government. 'Olwi Mostafa 'Eleiwa and 'Esām al-Qamari and others joined us afterwards. This cell expanded to its best in 1974 and 1975. In 1975, there was a division within the cell, as 'Eleiwa questioned the cell's approach and left it. A number of other dissidents from the cell joined the Technical Academy Cell. But Isma'eel Tantāwi, Mohamed 'Abdel Raheem and I continued with our cell. At the end of 1975, Tantāwi traveled to Germany, so I started recruiting cadres for the cell. There were also members that Mohamed 'Abdel Raheem recruited. One of the people that I recruited for my cell was Nabeel al-Bora'i, my brother Mohamed Rabee' al-Zawahiri, Sayyid Imām 'Abdel 'Azeez, Mohamed Mostafa Shalabi and 'Esām Hasheesh. I also recruited more members from Maadi through Nabeel al-Bora'i, including Waheed Gamāl al-Deen, Khāled Medhat al-Fiqi, Khāled 'Abdel Samee', Hassan 'Ali and his friend Tāriq. I don't remember his last name. There were other new recruits from Maadi including a student at a faculty of veterinary medicine called 'Esām, and Yusef 'Abdel Mageed, a technical staff sergeant in the air force, as well as Yusef Riādh, a student at the Faculty of Agronomy at Al-Azhar University.

Mohamed 'Abdel Raheem had recruited a number of cadres in his cell, but I never asked him about them. I only remember one person called Abu al-Hassan. He studied with 'Abdel Raheem at the Faculty of Engineering, 'Ein Shams University, and used to live in Shubra. There were two others from the Faculty of Engineering, 'Ein Shams University. One of them as far as I remember was called Mahmūd. I don't remember the rest of his name. Mohamed 'Abdel Raheem told me that he recruited a number of young people a month ago and that he is looking after them. Over the last two years, I have recruited Ameen Yusef al-Domeiri, while my brother Mohamed who now lives in Saudi Arabia succeeded in recruiting two Egyptians working there, Mostafa Kāmel Mostafa and 'Abdel Hādi al-Tunsi. A number of members broke away from our cell, including Waheed Gamāl al-Deen, Tāriq, Hassan 'Ali and Yusef Riādh.

Before I was arrested I was the leader of the cell and the members were Mohamed 'Abdel Raheem, Sayyid Imām 'Abdel 'Azeez, Ameen al-Domeiri, Nabeel al-Boraʻi, Khāled Medhat al-Fiqi, Khāled ʻAbdel Sameeʻ and the three members in Saudi Arabia including my brother Mohamed. About a month or two ago, a member from my cell Ameen al-Domeiri met a member from ʻAbbūd al-Zomor's cell. This person is most probably Tāriq al-Zomor. This encounter led to an agreement between our cell and Zomor's to have some cooperation. An example of this cooperation is that ʻAbbūd al-Zomor's cell stored a machine gun and some explosives at Ameen al-Domeiri's place. Also, when ʻAbbūd al-Zomor was on the run and needed a furnished apartment to hide in, Ameen al-Domeiri found an apartment for him. Domeiri also gave Zomor EÊ800 from our cell's financial resources, which I gave to Domeiri, to buy speakers because it was part of his plan to go on demonstrations in different squares using speakers after assassinating the president of the republic and delivering a statement on the radio. Zomor also gave Domeiri some explosives on October 12, 1981 to hold on to.

My relationship with Zomor started after the assassination on October 6, 1981, when I visited him at 10 o'clock p.m. in the apartment in Haram[8] where he was hiding. I went there with Domeiri and Sayyid Imām ʻAbdel ʻAzeez in the latter's car. ʻAbdel ʻAzeez and I stayed in the car, while Domeiri went to his apartment and brought him to meet us. I had a discussion with Zomor on two issues. First, I told him that the assassination was enough and that he should not develop it into a full-scale battle with the government. Second, I asked him if he knew a major at the army called ʻEsām al-Qamari and whether an officer called Gamāl Rasheed was one of the people who implemented the assassination. I also asked him whether the assassins directly follow him. He answered that he knows neither ʻEsām al-Qamari, nor Gamāl Rasheed, and that the people who executed the assassination follow him directly.

I met Zomor three times afterwards. The second time I met him was one or two days after our first encounter. I went with ʻEsām al-Qamari and Domeiri, in the latter's car. During this meeting inside Domeiri's car in front of the apartment where he stayed, Qamari asked Zomor whether Gamāl Rasheed took part in the assassination. Zomor answered that he did not. Qamari also asked him whether he was planning, as he heard, to target the people in Sadāt's funeral. Zomor said he was thinking about that. Then Qamari said that he was thinking about launching a coup by attacking the Republican Guards[9] with a battalion of tanks, but Zomor told him that this military action was not well planned. I forgot to mention that Qamari had a codename, Zakariyya, which is the name that Zomor knew. When Zomor saw Qamari, he recognized him as the officer who escaped from the army after the authorities knew about his connections with Islamic movements.

The third time, we were supposed to meet Qamari in the Kit Kat Square on October 11, 1981 and then go together to Zomor's apartment. But we did not manage to meet Qamari. So Domeiri and I went to Zomor's apartment without him. This was the first time I had ever been inside his apartment. We sat in the room at the end of the apartment. We had a discussion about the Assyūt operation, which took place two days after the assassination of Sadāt. I told him that the losses of the Assyūt operation, in which they attacked the Assyūt Security Administration Building, outweighed its gains. We agreed with Zomor to meet him the following day with Qamari on October 12, 1981. Zomor had asked Qamari to get him ten hand grenades and two pistols in our previous meeting, which I have mentioned earlier. During this third meeting, there were about three people in the apartment with Zomor, as well as someone who was sleeping, whom Zomor called Tāriq. Then Zomor asked all of them to leave the room and stay in another room. I don't know any of these four people and I did not know what Zomor told them before Domeiri and I arrived because they were asked to leave as soon as we got there.

The fourth and last meeting with Zomor was when Domeiri, Qamari and I went to his hideaway in Haram on October 12, 1981. This time Qamari had brought him the hand grenades he had requested. I do not know how many he gave him. Qamari, Domeiri, Zomor and I stayed in a room for a whole hour. During this meeting, Zomor gave Domeiri and Qamari some explosives, including dynamites. He also gave Qamari two small boxes with bullets caliber 7.65mm and some bullets caliber 9mm. I don't remember the number of bullets he gave him. Zomor started explaining how he makes hand grenades and how to use them. Qamari told Zomor that he came up with a way to make a time detonator for explosives. He said that he could make an electric circuit and use the timer of a fan and a broken light bulb buried in the powder of fireworks. Qamari tried to demonstrate his idea practically, but the detonator exploded by mistake and there was a loud bang. So Zomor walked into the balcony to see if anyone has noticed the explosion and then someone came from another room in the apartment to enquire about what happened. Zomor told him to say that a chair fell on the floor if asked. Afterwards, we left Zomor's place and gave Qamari a lift to an apartment in Giza that he had rented through Domeiri two months earlier or more, after I had introduced Domeiri to Qamari, without telling the former that the latter was a fugitive officer. But Domeiri eventually discovered this himself when I went with Qamari to Domeiri's pharmacy to go to Zomor's. I had told Domeiri that a fugitive officer wanted to meet Zomor to ask about an officer called Gamāl Rasheed, and whether he took part in the assassination or not.

I first met Qamari in February or March of this year, through Mohamed 'Abdel Raheem, who told me that Qamari had a cell in the army that is planning to topple the government to establish an Islamic state. He also told me that he wanted our group to cooperate with Qamari's. 'Abdel Raheem came to my house with Qamari. They were carrying two bags that 'Abdel Raheem told me were full of ammunition that Qamari brought from the army, but he did not have a place to hide it. He wanted me to keep it as a kind of cooperation between our cell and Qamari's. Later on, Mohamed 'Abdel Raheem brought me a suitcase full of items including military books, land mines, hand grenades and maps of the positions of the Republican Guards and told me that 'Esām al-Qamari wanted to hide them because he realized that he was being watched. I hid all of the suitcase items, except for the suitcase itself, in an apartment that we had rented for the cell in Dār al-Salām[10] under Hassan 'Ali's name. Then I gave the suitcase to Hassan 'Ali to take to the apartment. The suitcase was seized by the authorities when 'Ali was walking on the street, but he managed to escape. Later on, Qamari told me that there were more explosives in Imbāba[11] that he needed to give us to hide. Domeiri and I went in a Fiat 124, met Qamari in Kit Kat[12] and left him the car. He was there with someone called Nabeel Na'eem. He has another name, al-Sayyid something. We agreed that they would drive the car to get the explosives to give to Domeiri and me. We said we would wait for them near Kit Kat Square because Qamari wouldn't allow us to accompany him to the Imbāba apartment. He did not want anyone to know where it was. About an hour later, they came back with the explosives, which Domeiri and I took to my apartment in Maadi, where I kept it for 10 to 15 days. During this period, I told Hassan 'Ali that I wanted to move these explosives to his apartment, but he told me that his apartment had become dangerous and that he wanted to move the other explosives and ammunitions that were already there. Sayyid Imām 'Abdel 'Azeez and I went to the Dār al-Salām apartment and took the explosives and ammunition from there to Nabeel al-Bora'i's apartment. Then I moved all the rest of the explosives from my apartment to his in two visits in 'Abdel 'Azeez's car. We stored all these explosives for 'Esām al-Qamari as a way of cooperation with his cell, which aimed at toppling the regime, using these explosives. A member from our cell, Khāled 'Abdel Samee', brought us some bullets and hand grenades from his relative in the army. I don't know his relative's name. We stored them too in Bora'i's apartment. As for the dynamite and other explosives that 'Abbūd al-Zomor gave to Domeiri in their last meeting just before the former was arrested, Domeiri gave them to 'Abdel 'Azeez, along with two pistols and two hand grenades. 'Abdel 'Azeez and I moved these things to an apartment owned by 'Abdel 'Azeez's sister on Road 106, Maadi. I have told the police about the apartment's location.

I also want to add that Nabeel al-Bora'i's mother owns a plot of land near the Bahbeet village in 'Ayyāt. I suggested that we should build an apartment, a barn and a warehouse, as well as a fence around it to use it as a sheep farm and a hideaway for our cell's members when need arises or for storing weapons, provided that one of us lives there permanently. This apartment is still under construction and it has not been used yet. The buildings were financed from the cell's money. It has cost E£2,700 so far. There is another apartment in Haram near Domeiri's pharmacy. He paid some money up front for the place from the cell's money. It is still under construction and we have not yet used it. There is also a warehouse that Ameen al-Domeiri rented near his pharmacy, where he was hiding some of the weapons that he received from Zomor. Domeiri told the police about the warehouse after he was arrested. They raided it, seizing the weapons. As for the financing of our cell, it was self-financed in part through donations and subscriptions from members. Such sources, however, were not sufficient. When my brother traveled to Saudi Arabia at the end of 1976, he put aside part of his salary, which he used to send us; and so did his other two friends who were also working in Saudi Arabia. My brother Mohamed called a friend of ours named Sālem 'Azzām in London and asked him for money to use against the Egyptian government. So he sent $1,000 to my brother, who then forwarded them to me. I prepared a memo about the cell's ideology and its objectives and distributed it internally amongst the members. But when I learnt that some members of religious groups were arrested, I burnt it. Mohamed 'Abdel Raheem had a copy of this memorandum. Our cell was not responsible for the assassination of the president of the republic. On the contrary, we did our best to prevent the situation from escalating, by urging 'Abbūd al-Zomor not to clash with the government any further. However, I was informed by Domeiri about the assassination at nine o'clock in the morning of October 6, but I was not convinced that it was a good idea.'

Then the interrogator had the following discussion with Zawahiri:
Question: When did you start getting interested in religious matters?
Answer: When I was in high school in 1965 or 1966, when I started reading religious books and following the Muslim Brothers' incident of 1965.[13] Some people started talking to me about why it was necessary for Muslim youths to get together. They said that the incident was directed solely against Islam. I was convinced.

The Road to Al-Qaeda

Question: When did the idea of forming the cell that you were in start?

Answer: Approximately 1966 or 1967.

Question: Whose idea was it to form this cell?

Answer: It was a group of students from the Maadi High School, as well as students from other schools including Isma'eel Tantāwi.

Question: Who established this cell?

Answer: A student called 'Adil al-'Ayyāt started the idea. Then Isma'eel Tantāwi, Sayyid Hanafi, 'Adil al-'Ayyāt and I established it, but 'Ayyāt withdrew early on.

Question: Did you name this cell?

Answer: No.

Question: What was the hierarchy of this cell?

Answer: Isma'eel Tantāwi was the leader. The rest were regular members, namely Sayyid Hanafi and I. After that, 'Olwy Mostafa 'Eleiwa joined us. The cell was growing rapidly until 1974, when some members left it.

Question: What was the purpose of this cell?

Answer: We wanted to establish an Islamic government.

Question: What does an Islamic government mean according to this cell?

Answer: A government that rules according to the *shari'a* of God Almighty.

The district attorney asked Zawahiri again in page 56 of the interrogations:

Question: What is the meaning of "jihad" according to your cell?

Answer: "Jihad" means removing the current government through resisting it and changing the current regime to establish an Islamic government instead.

Question: How would you replace the current government with an Islamic one?

Answer: Through a military coup. We were convinced that civilians and the military should cooperate to achieve this end.

Question: Why did you want to remove the current government?

Answer: Because it does not rule according to the *shari'a* of God, glorified be His name.

At the end of this session, the State security district attorney Mahmūd Mas'ūd asked whether they made sufficient arrangements towards their goal. Zawahiri answered that they tried, but they had much further to go, but were limited by insufficient resources.

In another interrogation session on December 2, 1981, Mahmūd Mas'ūd asked Zawahiri about the cell that he, Isma'eel Tantāwi, Sayyid Hanafi and 'Adil al-'Ayyāt established. Zawahiri answered:

In the beginning, the cell was made up of me, Isma'eel Tantāwi, Sayyid Hanafi, 'Adil al-'Ayyāt, 'Ali Sa'd, a man called Badr from Maadi, Yehia Hāshim and 'Abdel 'Azeem 'Azzām. Then Isma'eel Tantāwi, Sayyid Hanafi and I broke away from this cell, as every one of them left it. So the three of us formed our own cell. 'Olwi Mostafa 'Eleiwa, Mohamed 'Abdel Raheem, 'Esām al-Qamari and many others joined the cell afterwards. In 1974, the cell had about 40 members, before some members started breaking away, including 'Eleiwa. The cell became restricted to me, Isma'eel Tantāwi and Mohamed 'Abdel Raheem. Some people joined us later, while others left, until we reached the current 11 members, led by me. The members include Ameen al-Domeiri, Sayyid Imām 'Abdel 'Azeez, Nabeel al-Bora'i, Mohamed 'Abdel Raheem, Khāled Medhat al-Fiqi, Khāled 'Abdel Samee', Yusef 'Abdel Mageed, in addition to the three who are living in Saudi Arabia, namely my brother Mohamed, Mostafa Kāmel Mostafa and 'Abdel Hādi al-Tunsi. There was also a member called 'Esām. I do not remember his last name, but I remember that he was a student at a faculty of veterinary medicine.

Question: When did these members join the cell and how did they join?

Answer: Ameen al-Domeiri joined the cell about two years ago. Sayyid Imām 'Abdel 'Azeez introduced me to him. I asked him to join my cell and he agreed. Sayyid Imām 'Abdel 'Azeez joined the cell in 1975 or 1976 when he was training with me to be a practicing doctor at the Qasr al-'Einy Hospital, after finishing our last year of medical school. I was the one who recruited him as well. Nabeel al-Bora'i was in the first cell. Then he rejoined my cell in 1974 or 1975 and I was the one who renewed his membership. Mohamed 'Abdel Raheem was with me since the inception of the cell, while Khāled Medhat al-Fiqi was recruited through Nabeel al-Bora'i about three years ago. Khāled 'Abdel Samee' was recruited about two years ago by Waheed Gamāl al-Deen, but the former left the cell later. Yusef 'Abdel Mageed was recruited by Nabeel al-Bora'i about three years ago. 'Esām was also recruited about one and a half years ago by Nabeel al-Bora'i. My brother Mohamed has been in the cell since its inception. My brother Mohamed recruited Mostafa about three years ago and 'Abdel Hādi al-Tunsi about a year ago.

Question: What was the objective of establishing this cell?

Answer: We were trying to topple the regime by force to establish an Islamic government.

In page 62 of the interrogations, Zawahiri explains his approach that centers on launching a coup:

> Our objective for the first phase was to recruit the biggest possible number of civilians, as well as cooperating with military people. But the coup is a technical issue that should be planned by one of the military people who will join our cell.

This shows very clearly that Zawahiri had always believed in the necessity of a coup, as the only way to effect change and to establish an Islamic government. He also believed that preaching would not be effective, because without an Islamic government, there would be no way to change the people. Thus, for him, changing people and establishing an Islamic government were inextricable.

The following questions underline this significant element of Zawahiri's ideology:

Question: What do you think of the ruling system?

Answer: It is not completely in line with Islamic *shari'a*.

Question: What is the difference between this system and Islamic *shari'a*?

Answer: There are so many differences. For example, alcohol is legal, as are nightclubs and gambling. The government does not institute the legal Islamic punishments.

Question: How can Islamic *shari'a* be instituted the right way to avoid failure?

Answer: The government has to abide by Islamic *shari'a* in its laws and dealings and the people have to abide by Islamic *shari'a* in their behavior.

Question: How should the government be changed to the Islamic way? And how can the people be changed?

Answer: Through teaching the people the principles of Islam.

Zawahiri's way of thinking can lead us to an explanation of the style of government that the Taliban[14] movement established in Afghanistan after seizing control of most of the Afghan lands in 1996. There is a great similarity between his views and those of the Taliban. They demanded that secular and morally unacceptable television programs be replaced with sanctioned alternatives. When replacements were not found, they went so far as to issue presidential decrees banning any transmissions at all. They also issued decrees to make it illegal for women not to cover their heads and men not to grow their beards. The late Ahmed al-Naggār said that Islamic Jihad was influenced deeply by the ascent to power of the Taliban. Naggār is a leading figure in the Nahia flank of the group. His involvement dates back to the Jihad case, in which he was sentenced to three years in prison. He was later sentenced to death in absentia in the Khān al-Khalili case in 1997.[15] He was executed in 2000 after his arrest in Albania. Islamic Jihad defended the Taliban against criticism regarding the government's stand against educating women and the closing of schools, and continued to defend them when they began preventing women from going to work. According to Naggār, Islamic Jihad literature defended the Taliban by explaining that they only suspended the educational process pending changes in syllabi. They also claimed that the group prevented women from working only until more suitable job opportunities arose, suggesting that it was only a temporary stage. "It is very clear that the Islamic Jihad supports the Taliban wholeheartedly," Naggār concluded.

Zawahiri's efforts to create links with people in the army should attest to his intention, from the first day he joined a clandestine cell, to topple the government and to establish an Islamic state. Zawahiri does not like to take risks when he is not ready. He wouldn't choose to get involved in clashes with the government that might inflict losses on his cell. Based on this logic, he tried to dissuade 'Abbūd al-Zomor from continuing the clashes with the government that were being planned after the assassination of Sadāt. He visited Zomor in his hideaway on the evening of October 6, 1981, accompanied by Ameen al-Domeiri and Sayyid Imām 'Abdel 'Azeez. "I told him [Zomor] that he should not continue his clashes with the government and that he should be content with the assassination of the president of the republic," Zawahiri said.

On page 98 of the interrogations, Zawahiri shows the difference between his cell and other cells when he says:

We agree with the majority of Muslims and the four imāms.[16] We are different from the Takfir wal Hijra group,[17] as we do not consider people infidels because of their sins. And we are different from the Muslim Brotherhood because sometimes they do not oppose the government.

Some people might doubt the information in his confessions because they were extracted under unnatural circumstances, but what he said 16 years after his time in prison dissipates any doubts. In an interview with the French news agency Agence France-Presse (AFP) in 1997, he was asked whether he was against any initiative to stop the military conflict between his group and the Egyptian regime; Zawahiri answered, "The military conflict and all other kinds of resistance whether ideological or on the media level between the *mujāhideen* [jihad fighters] who are the vanguards of Islamic awakening and the regime will stop when the regime hands the rule to Muslims."

3

Afghanistan: Land of Jihad

The well-known lawyer Mahfūz 'Azzām, Zawahiri's maternal uncle, once told me, "You always claim that Zawahiri's approach was a violent one, with a coup as its objective. I disagree with you. I am not so quick to describe Zawahiri's approach as violent and set on launching a coup."

'Azzām is a man trained in the law and one of the heads of the 'Azzām family, Zawahiri's mother's family. For this reason, he believes that the court ruling of 1984, which acquitted Zawahiri of any accusation, is sufficient to disprove my theory. It must be noted, however, that the court also turned down the results of investigations that said that he was the leader of a cell. Based on the rulings alone, it would seem that the court was completely convinced that all the accusations against him were baseless except for the unlicensed possession of a pistol, a comparatively minor offense which carries a sentence of only three years.

Another reason for 'Azzām's belief that Zawahiri's ideology was not centered on the idea of a coup is the content of the papers of case no. 462 of 1981. According to the papers, immediately after the assassination of Sadāt, Zawahiri had hurried to meet 'Abbūd al-Zomor in his hideaway in Haram. There he is said to have snapped at him, "You don't have any excuse to kill the people in the Assyūt Security Administration building. I don't agree with that." The difference between my assessment of Zawahiri's ideology and 'Azzām's, is that mine is an historical account of his ideology as an old leader in the *jihādi* movement, while 'Azzām's was influenced by his relation to him, as well as his job as a lawyer defending Zawahiri in the Jihad case. His evaluation of his nephew's ideology is a belittlement of Zawahiri. We also disagreed about the reason for Zawahiri's decision not to return to Egypt. 'Azzām thinks that the circumstances that followed Sadāt's assassination prevented him from returning. Specifically, Zawahiri refused to return to the torture he suffered in prison after he was arrested in October, 1981, and to the accusing fingers that were pointed at him. 'Azzām mentioned that Zawahiri kept his clinic in Maadi and paid its rising lease for years, hoping to eventually come back and lead a normal life.

I ask 'Azzām and Zawahiri's family to allow me to disagree with them on this point in particular. Zawahiri left Egypt on purpose and so did many other leaders and members of the Islamic movements, after they were released in the Jihad case. Afghanistan was the best place for them to settle because it offered them what they were seeking: fighting and jihad.[1]

Zawahiri could not have stayed in Egypt after the authorities discovered his activities, as he relied mainly upon their remaining secret. An important component of his approach was recruitment of cadres from the military, very selectively. This was because he was convinced that a military coup was the best way to bring about change with the least possible losses. When his plans were discovered, he fell under the eyes of the authorities, bringing an end to the clandestine approach he preferred.

An anecdote that demonstrates the persistence of Zawahiri's desire to travel relates to his work permit situation. When he decided to travel, the authorities would not grant him approval of the work permit that he needed to be able to leave the country. Tricky and shrewd as he is, Zawahiri presented his passport to a tourist agency and got a visa to travel to Tunisia as a tourist in order to leave Egypt. After arriving in Tunisia, he left for Jeddah where he worked for the Ibn al-Nāfees Hospital for a few months. Then he went to Pakistan and from there he managed to enter the land of jihad: Afghanistan.

Another reason that Zawahiri did not return to Egypt is that, through the pain of torture, he was forced to confess against his friends, followers and disciples. He even tipped the police off about the whereabouts of one of his best friends 'Esām al-Qamari. Zawahiri might have thought that his leadership had lost its credibility in the eyes of his disciples because of this. In his last book, he did not mention these confessions or helping the police arrest Qamari. However, he did refer to it in passing when he spoke about Qamari and the reasons why he was arrested.

It is important to mention Zawahiri's confessions about the arrest of Qamari in the interrogations of the Higher State Security case no. 462 of 1981. On page 3 of the confessions, he says,

I was arrested the day before yesterday on Friday at around 11:30 a.m., while I was walking on Nahda Street in Maadi. The State Security police asked me to inform them where 'Esām al-Qamari was because he is my friend. Since I knew that Qamari was hiding in a turnery workshop in Manshiet Nasser, Gamāliyya, I told the police, who took me there to show them the place and then they took me away. So I did not see what happened. On the morning of the same day, Qamari had phoned me at home and asked to meet me at 5:30 p.m. in a small mosque near the Kit Kat Square, where we used to meet. The police asked me to go to this mosque to meet him so that they could arrest him because they were worried that there would be loss of lives. I went with them to the mosque and sat there under their eyes until he arrived and while he was performing the mosque greeting prayers he was arrested.

On page 28, Zawahiri talks about the circumstances surrounding the arrest of one of the members of his cell, Nabeel al-Bora'i. Asked by the interrogator about the period of time over which Bora'i had harbored a certain stock of explosives and ammunitions, he said, "From as soon as they [the explosives and ammunitions] were sent to him in June of last year, until he was arrested two days ago, when I informed the police."

What was most difficult and what caused Zawahiri profound psychological and moral pain was that in the session of the Higher Military Court held on December 6, 1981, he was brought to testify against Qamari and his fellow officers, 'Abdel 'Aziz al-Gamāl, 'Awny 'Abdel Mageed, Sayyid 'Abbās and Gamāl Rasheed.

The military court asked him about his relationship with Qamari. He answered, "I first met Major 'Esām al-Qamari in February 1981 and I

The Road to Al-Qaeda

met him regularly until I was arrested in October 1981." The court asked him about the nature of their relationship. Zawahiri said that he knew that Qamari had escaped from the army and that I was helping him.

He occasionally visited me in my clinic. I also found a flat for him and gave him money and the seized pistol, along with other weapons including five pistols, two machine guns and a number of bullets, I do not remember how many.

He gave the court more information about the activities of Qamari and 'Abdel 'Aziz al-Gamāl.

Surely, the only reason for Zawahiri's confessions was the terrible physical and moral torture that he suffered. Although he has an excuse for his confessions according to Islamic *fiqh* [the science of Islamic law], he still felt very bitter and could not recover quickly from this experience, which is capable of shaking a leader like him. He preferred to leave Egypt and he knew his destination. He had already visited Afghanistan in 1980 and worked in the Sayyida Zeinab Hospital, which belongs to the Muslim Brotherhood's Islamic Medical Society, when he was asked to be part of the medical group that went there to provide medical services to Afghans. It was a good chance for him to see on the ground this huge field for jihad. He knew from that first time he set foot in Afghanistan that it was the ideal place for jihad.

Many people have drawn a distinction between Zawahiri's skills in oration and rhetoric and those of his close ally Osāma bin Lāden. They said that bin Lāden has the ability to reach to the hearts of people with simple words, and is a much better orator than Zawahiri. It may be true that Zawahiri is a less gifted orator than bin Lāden. However, Zawahiri is gifted in individual persuasion and in recruiting new cadres, because his ideas are very organized and his aims are clear. Moreover, the cause that bin Lāden talks about – namely the American presence in the Gulf region, and the American role in supporting the Zionists in Palestine – has been his main concern for many years. It is natural that bin Lāden's words are more eloquent when he is talking about his central concern. Zawahiri now speaks on these issues as a result of his coalition with bin Lāden under cruel circumstances, so they are new to him. Thus it is natural for Zawahiri's oratorical skills to appear weaker than those of bin Lāden.

Zawahiri is a shrewd planner. He made the whole world think that he was living in Switzerland by announcing that he would hold an international press conference in a hotel in Geneva in 1993, in a fax that he sent to the *Al-Hayat*[2] newspaper correspondent in Cairo. But later on, he sent another statement canceling the press conference and claiming that he had discovered that the Egyptian authorities were planning to assassinate him. A few years later, it turned out that when he was getting ready to leave Afghanistan to go to Sudan and Yemen he spread these rumors about his whereabouts as a trick to assure his peaceful travel.

Al-Qaeda in Afghanistan

Zawahiri expressed his desire to leave Egypt and settle in Afghanistan immediately after he was arrested and accused in the Jihad case, following the assassination of Sadāt. He had visited the country twice in relief operations in 1980 and 1981. He stayed there for six months, during which time he had a good chance to become familiar with the place. He wrote in his last book,

> Through my experience in the Afghan battlefield for jihad since 1980, I have realized how valuable this struggle is to the Islamic *umma* in general, and to the *jihādi* movement in particular. I have realized how important it is to make use of this setting. That is why, after living there for four months in my first visit then leaving, I returned to Afghanistan in March 1981. On that trip I stayed for another two months, then had to return to Egypt for pressing reasons. There I was imprisoned for three years, my sentence ending in 1984. I could not return to the Afghan jihad battlefield until mid 1986. Through my ties and dealings with the people on the ground, I discovered a number of very dangerous facts. The most important of these is that the movement is in need of a land that can better serve as the soil where its seeds can grow and gain experience in fighting, politics and the organization of cells.

Afghanistan was to Zawahiri the only way out of the dilemma in which he found himself after the discovery of his cell in Egypt in 1981. It was also easier for him to recruit and train cadres in Afghanistan, away from the watchful eyes of the authorities who were in constant pursuit. Also, it was to his benefit to escape the intellectual openness in Egypt, where his approach could be questioned. In an open society like Egypt, the media critiques not only those in power, but also those within the different factions of the Islamic movement itself. Afghan society, on the other hand, is very closed because of the war against the Soviets. This history also made it a more suitable environment for preparing Muslim youths for the long-awaited battle with the power that has now become the sole great power in the world: the United States. He also had more resources there for the attacks on the Egyptian government that he intended to coordinate by sending cadres from Afghanistan. Thus he could use his presence in Afghanistan to implement such operations inside Egypt.

Some people might argue that Zawahiri was not involved in any of the operations that were performed by members of his cell in Egypt, because he was not accused in the cases in which members from his cell were accused. These include trials following the failed assassination attempts on the former interior minister Hassan al-Alfi[3] and the former prime minister 'Atef Sidqi,[4] as well as other cases. Other observers believe that the Egyptian authorities avoided charging him for other reasons. These hearings were held before a military court that the European Union countries do not recognize, at a time when it was believed that Zawahiri was living in Geneva. A sentence of death in absentia might have enabled him to seek asylum abroad. It is possible that he was not charged precisely because the Egyptian government feared that scenario, in which the death sentence would effectively have allowed him to live legally anywhere in the world.

Defenders of Zawahiri might also argue that he does not deserve the sentence of death in absentia issued by the Egyptian authorities in 1998 in the case known as the Returnees from Albania case. The argument is that the decision holds no sway because he was not there to defend himself. Another reason why the Egyptian authorities did not accuse him at first is that the members that implemented earlier operations were so strong that they did not make any confessions that implicated their leader. Those involved in the Returnees from Albania case, on the other hand, gave detailed confessions about Zawahiri's leadership of the group. There are a number of explanations for why the group accused in the Returnees from Albania case gave in and made confessions about their leader. First, there was a general feeling of frustration among the members due to a number of foiled operations inside Egypt in the period that followed the bombing of the two American embassies in Nairobi and Darussalam in 1998. This frustration was deepened by their arrest outside of Egypt in Albania, which was an unpleasant and unexpected surprise. Also, prominent Islamic Jihad leader Ahmed Salāma Mabrūk, Zawahiri's right-hand man, was arrested. In his possession, the authorities found a laptop that had many names of the members of the Egyptian Islamic Jihad. This led to the arrest of more than a hundred members, who were tried in one case. Zawahiri's family, however, believes that he never committed a crime in his whole life, whether before 1981 or in 1999. His uncle Mahfūz 'Azzām argues that the military court which issued the sentence in the Returnees from Albania case should not have made rulings on civilians. He also rejects the sentence because it was in absentia, with no opportunity for the accused to defend himself. He goes on to emphasize that no European countries recognize military courts, which is why they have given political asylum to many of those who were sentenced by them.

Members of Zawahiri's family see him as a man who stands by his beliefs. They feel that his participation in resisting, and in urging people to resist oppression and occupation in Afghanistan and Palestine is the fulfillment of the religious duty to engage in jihad. They do not accept the theory that he was involved in the attacks on the United States. According to 'Azzām, because he is not a military leader and did not receive any studies related to flying, he would have been unable to plan and supervise an operation the size of the September 11 attacks.

Out of Afghanistan

After Zawahiri built his group in Afghanistan, the *mujāhideen* [literally "jihad fighters," here refers to the multiple factions in Afghanistan, including natives and immigrants, who cooperate to fight the enemies of Islam] entered Kabul in 1992, where Sibghatullah Mujadadi was appointed interim president for the *mujāhideen* government. Mujadadi tried to turn his interim government into a permanent one, but his attempts found great opposition from the rest of the *mujāhideen*, especially Burhanuddin Rabbani and his strong ally Ahmed Shah Mas'ūd, as well as Gulbuddin Hekmatyar. Mujadadi sent messages to the international community, especially Pakistan and Arab countries, that he did not want the Arab Afghans [also called Arab *mujāhideen*, these are Arabs who migrated to Afghanistan to participate in jihad] to stay in the country after their mission had been accomplished. This was a political gesture that was meant to placate some Arab countries such as Egypt and Algeria, who were concerned that their citizens would use Afghanistan as a launch pad for attacks on their home countries. Egypt had already started taking security measures against the Arab Afghans by trying them before military courts in absentia and issuing harsh sentences, including death sentences for the elite of the Arab Afghans, as well as sentences of life imprisonment for others.

The crisis of Arab Afghans increased when Burhanuddin Rabbani became president, because *mujāhideen* factions were still fighting, but the Arab Afghans refused to be part of the struggle because they did not trust the intentions of the leaders of any of the factions. They were worried that they would be used as pawns in the struggle. The fears of Arab Afghan leaders skyrocketed when Pakistan extradited a number of Egyptian fundamentalists to the Egyptian government, notable among whom was Mohamed 'Abdel Raheem al-Sharqāwi. Sharqāwi had established the first clandestine *jihādi* cell along with Zawahiri in 1968. He was later accused with Zawahiri in the Jihad case, and was sentenced to three years in the Tora Prison. After his release, at the end of 1984, he traveled with Zawahiri.

Yemen and Sudan: temporary stages

Eventually, the Afghan leaders turned from *mujāhideen* to warlords against Zawahiri, bin Lāden and other Arab Afghan leaders. This and other events in Afghanistan prompted many of the Arab Afghani leaders to flee the country, heading for Sudan and Yemen. Osāma bin Lāden invested his money in huge agricultural projects in Sudan, which was then suffering from a grinding economic crisis. His money gave him political weight, which allowed him to host other Arab Afghan leaders such as Zawahiri, Tharwat Salāh Shehāta and Abu 'Obayda al-Bensheery, who later drowned in Lake Victoria at the end of 1995.

Renowned leader Ahmed Ibrahim al-Naggār, who was executed in the year 2000, escaped from Egypt in 1993. This was after the Egyptian authorities arrested the Vanguards of Conquest, a group affiliated with Islamic Jihad. The leaders of Islamic Jihad managed to provide him with all the resources he needed to flee the country. He related:

'Adil al-Sudāni [who was later executed in 1998 in connection with the Khān al-Khalili case] told me that he would get me out of the country on a passport in someone else's name. Sure enough, he brought me someone's passport named 'Abdel Raheem Mohamed Hussein and took my pictures. He bought me a ticket for the ferry from Nuwaiba' and told me to go to Jordan, take the bus to Amman and go to the Jordan River Hotel. He told me that some people would call me at the hotel. I left on October 18, 1993 and went to the Jordan River Hotel. I did not know who was going to call me. The next day I received a call from Mahmūd al-Deeb [one of the leaders of Islamic Jihad in Kerdasa, Giza, who was later killed in a battle with the Egyptian authorities after his return from Afghanistan in 1997]. Deeb called me from Yemen and told me to book a plane ticket to meet him there. I informed him of my departure and arrival dates. I left on October 23, 1993 and when I arrived in the Sanaa Airport, I found him waiting for me. He took me to an area called Al-Sawad in the southern part of Sanaa, where we went to a one-story house. As soon as I entered the house, I realized it belonged to some young people from the group who live in Yemen. Many leaders from Islamic Jihad visited me there, such as Morgān Sālem, Mohamed al-Zawahiri, Ahmed Salāma Mabrūk, Tharwat Salāh Shehāta. All of them came to make sure that the other members were all right and to welcome me. During my stay in the house, I learned that these young people were members of the group that received their military training in Afghanistan, where they participated in the Afghan War. I also learned that the leaders of the group took refuge in Yemen, where they could hide their members and continue the activities of the group. The group that I was staying with required only that I receive jurisprudence lessons from Mohamed Sharaf. After a while of staying in this house, I was informed by Deeb that the group uses Sanaa as a place to train some members that would later be sent to Egypt to perform their operations, while the Yemeni city of Ta'izz was the place where the members were sent after they had been prepared and were ready for operations inside Egypt.

On page 20 of the confessions of Naggār, he says that the Arab Afghans left Afghanistan after Kabul was opened in 1992.

What I understood during my stay in Yemen the first time is that it was a refuge that replaced Afghanistan after Pakistan started opposing the Arab presence. In response to this opposition, the group's members and leaders started looking for a more suitable place to stay and to continue their activities. The suitable places near Egypt included Yemen, Sudan and Jordan. But the best place was Yemen because of its large Egyptian community, and because it was inexpensive. Furthermore, at that point Yemen was suffering from the struggle between its northern and southern parts.

Sudan, on the other hand, did not offer many job opportunities, and it was expensive to live there. Furthermore, Naggār argues that the tribal make-up in Yemen was more suitable than that in Sudan for Islamic Jihad to operate freely. Sudan still attracted some leaders, such as Zawahiri. Naggār mentions an even more important factor that can explain to us what Zawahiri was thinking when he chose Sudan to be his base. "During my stay in Yemen, I cannot say there was any coordination between the Yemeni regime and the leaders of Islamic Jihad, unlike in Sudan, where there was coordination between the Sudanese government and the members of the group."

Zawahiri preferred Yemen as a launching pad for his activities, from which he could send the members to Egypt to perform armed operations. Still, he was forced to transfer his members from Yemen to Sudan following the failed attempt on the life of the former Egyptian prime minister 'Atef Sidqi.

Naggār describes his own move to Sudan:

In October 1994, Morgān Sālem called me and said that there were orders that I should go to Sudan. I bought a plane ticket and flew to Khartoum. In the airport, I was received by Morgān Sālem and Nasr Fahmi [the latter was killed in the American bombing of Afghanistan in December 2001]. They drove me to a three-story house in Khartoum in the Riyadh area. I stayed for one night on the ground floor with a number of young people. The next day, Morgān Sālem came and took me in a private car, along with Tharwat Salāh Shehāta, to meet Zawahiri in a house in Khartoum. I don't know exactly where the house was, but I remember an old, one-story house. It did not look like a house. It looked more like an office. During the meeting, I talked to Zawahiri in the presence of Morgān Sālem about the group's Civilian Committee and how he thought it should work in the future. He said that there should be a new style, especially after the Vanguards of Conquest case, and that the old information should be completely ignored.

Returning to Afghanistan

After the Taliban Movement took over Kabul, and ousted President Rabbani, Zawahiri saw a good opportunity to return to Afghanistan, the land that he loved. In Afghanistan, Zawahiri felt protected by the country's rugged and mountainous landscape. There he felt confident offering his followers intensive military, political and educational training. Naggār says that Zawahiri, his brother Mohamed, Ahmed Abu al-Kheir, Ahmed Salāma Mabrūk and Tharwat Salāh Shehāta headed for Afghanistan through Azerbaijan, after the Taliban opened its lands to the Arab *mujāhideen*. The Media Committee of Islamic Jihad had issued a brochure about the Taliban, in which it enumerated the

Taliban's virtues and mentioned its status as a religious fundamentalist movement led by a group of students of Islamic *shari'a*. It added that it was clear from early 1996 that Islamic Jihad was an ardent supporter of the Taliban. When the Taliban controlled 95 per cent of the Afghan lands, Osāma bin Lāden struck a deal with the Taliban leaders, including Mullah Mohamed 'Omar, who was described in some of the literature of Islamic Jihad as the "leader of the faithful." The deal allowed bin Lāden to remain in the lands controlled by the Taliban and to protect the well-being of Arab Afghans in those lands. The leaders of Islamic Jihad went back to Afghanistan and told other members to follow. Members of various Islamic groups based in Egypt and other Arab and Muslim countries headed for Afghanistan as well. None of these groups had the same status as Islamic Jihad in Afghanistan, as the latter signed an official alliance agreement with Osāma bin Lāden.

The Taliban did not try to force the Arab Afghans to fight against the other Afghan factions. Also, many Arab Afghans lived there without getting involved in Al-Qaeda [literally "the base"], which was the movement led by Osāma bin Lāden, or the Front that he established in February 1998.

4

Changes in Zawahiri's Ideology: The Near and Far Enemies

In the first years after he joined the "Islamic *jihādi* movement," as he used to call it, Ayman al-Zawahiri thought there was only one way to bring about change: toppling the government through a military coup. At a later stage, he started launching armed operations against top Egyptian government figures, although he had opposed this approach earlier when faced with 'Abbūd al-Zomor's plan to clash with the government after the assassination of President Anwar al-Sadāt. He asked Zomor to content himself with the assassination at that point. At the end of the 1980s, while he was in Afghanistan, and following some clashes between the Gamā'a al-Islāmiyya and the Egyptian government, Zawahiri objected to the attempts of the Gamā'a al-Islāmiyya to organize popular demonstrations against the government and the economic difficulties that affected many segments of Egyptian society. He explained that provoking the authorities would lead to tighter security arrangements and closer scrutiny of the members of the group, and eventually to the arrest of more members and the confiscation of weapons, which could otherwise be used in future operations.

Zawahiri's followers, mainly young people, urged him not to let the Gamā'a al-Islāmiyya be the only ones active in performing their jihad duty. They wanted to put the good military training they had received in Afghanistan to use, and Zawahiri yielded to their pressure. Contrary to his better judgment, he ordered his followers to perform armed operations against some of the top Egyptian figures. The first of these operations was the foiled assassination attempt on the former interior minister Hassan al-Alfi in 1993. A number of operations followed, including the assassination attempt on former prime minister 'Atef Sidqi, and then the assassination of the main witness in the Sidqi assassination, Sayyid Yehia. Zawahiri's group targeted Yehia for having informed the police about Al-Sayyid Salāh, the leader of the assassination attempt on Sidqi.

Zawahiri had consistently avoided confrontation with the authorities in order to facilitate preparations for a total coup. His wariness of high profile tactics had been reinforced by the experience of operating from outside Egypt. Clashes with the authorities led to increased difficulty recruiting members from the military as measures to prevent any Islamic infiltration were tightened. In Egypt, he faced increasing pressure to clash with the government from many of his followers who had just returned from fighting the Soviets in Afghanistan, and were ready to move their armed operations to Egypt to fight the regime. His followers pointed out that the Gamā'a al-Islāmiyya, though its resources were limited, had managed to launch several operations against top Egyptian government figures and economic institutions such as banks and the tourism industry. It was no secret that Zawahiri's close relationship with Sheikh Osāma bin Lāden provided him with significant financial resources, and his followers believed that these should enable Islamic Jihad to surpass the Gamā'a al-Islāmiyya in terms of armed operations against the regime in Egypt. Eventually, Zawahiri was persuaded to orchestrate temporary clashes with the Egyptian regime. This marked a significant change in his style.

Although the Arab–Israeli conflict is the central cause for the Arab and Islamic nation, it was a marginal issue for Zawahiri, and he put neither financial nor human support towards it. However, he did offer moral support. His moral and media support to this cause was clear in the condolences he sent after the death of Fathi al-Shaqāqi. He wrote:

Islamic Jihad in Egypt offers its condolences to our brother the martyr Dr. Fathi al-Shaqāqi. We ask God, glorified be His name, to accept his good deeds and his martyrdom, and we support his brethren in their jihad. We confirm to his brethren and to all *mujāhideen* that jihad is the way of martyrdom and that Fathi al-Shaqāqi deserves this honor. We have known him to be a true *mujāhid*, who combated

Changes in Zawahiri's Ideology   **61**

the Jews, refusing the treaties of humiliation and surrender. We ask God to support us on the road of jihad.

Zawahiri believed that the road to Jerusalem passes through Cairo and this was always his answer to why his group does not launch operations against the Jews in support of the operations implemented by the Palestinian Islamic Jihad and Hamās groups. He has always said that the only acceptable form of jihad is armed struggle and that any true Muslim should confront the internal enemy, or the "near enemy," and only after that the external enemy, or the "far enemy."

Zawahiri explained the idea of near enemy and far enemy in an article entitled, "The Way to Jerusalem Passes Through Cairo," published in *Al-Mujāhideen* in April, 1995. He wrote, "Jerusalem will not be opened[1] until the battles in Egypt and Algeria have been won and until Cairo has been opened," meaning that the main enemies are Muslim regimes, which do not rule according to Islamic *shari'a*.

Zawahiri was very critical of the calls for ceasing all armed operations against the regime in Egypt in order to get ready for the imminent confrontation with Israel. During the trial of Khāled Ibrahim, the leader of the Gamā'a al-Islāmiyya in Aswan, before the Higher State Security Court in April 1996, Ibrahim called on all members of Islamist movements in Egypt to stop all armed operations for a year. Many figures offered political and media support to Ibrahim's call. In the transcript of his speech, which was published the next day in the London-based *Al-Hayat*, Ibrahim said:

> From this sacred spot in this court, I call on the people of Egypt, especially the elite of this great nation, to stand like one man in the face of this black sedition. We should all combat this sedition by turning the blood that was shed through fighting between people of one nation into constructive work that can extend our civilization to the next epoch. These same people once participated in building the country's great glory that was established over centuries, when our beloved Egypt was the pearl of the East and the leader of the region. Let's turn these torn-off limbs into bricks that can build your glory and your fort to protect you from your many enemies,

especially Israel, supported by international Zionism, which dreams of rebuilding the Solomon's Temple and establishing a great empire for the Jews between the Nile and the Euphrates. There is also America that wants to draw a new international system which the whole world must follow.

Following Ibrahim's call, I issued a press statement, saying:

Our Muslim *umma* is surrounded by danger in the form of the trio: Zionism, crusaders and communism that are conspiring against it. The *umma* is at a very gloomy stage. Israel is still dreaming of its great state, and to achieve this, it sieges the *mujāhideen* in the occupied Arab territories and chases the soldiers of Hamās and Palestinian Islamic Jihad in Gaza, Jericho and the West Bank. It is also trying to liquidate Hizbullah in Lebanon, and has recently signed a strategic agreement with Turkey to bring Iran under siege. Meanwhile, the Golan Heights is still under occupation.

I stressed that such was our reality that allowed Israel to tamper with the Muslim *umma*. That is why I decided to address my message to the leaders of Islamic movements abroad to issue a decision to cease all armed operations. But Zawahiri considered Ibrahim's call and my ensuing support for it "media propaganda."

In a statement issued by Zawahiri on May 20, 1996, he rejected any intention to stop fighting the Egyptian regime, saying that the main mistake of the Gamā'a al-Islāmiyya was that it drew a distinction between the internal enemy and the outside enemy. He cited the distinction between the British and King Farouq, between the Americans and Gamāl 'Abdel Nasser in the early days of his rule and between the Soviets and Nasser later on in his era. He also cited the distinction between the Jews and Sadāt. He added that fighting the near enemy is prioritized because God says in the Koran, "Fight those of the disbelievers who are close to you."[2] He ended his statement by saying,

To conclude, you victorious people, do not give the regime a chance to buy time and do not dissuade Muslim youths in Egypt. They have

Changes in Zawahiri's Ideology   **63**

opened a new Front against Israel, as in the operation of the Europa Hotel[3] performed by the Gamā'a al-Islāmiyya, and in the Khān al-Khalili operation against Israeli tourists, even if in the end it was not destined to be implemented.

Zawahiri surprised the whole world in February 1998 by forming the International Islamic Front for Jihad on the Jews and Crusaders, a new organization under the leadership of Osāma bin Lāden. It issued a *fatwa* [an authoritative command or proclamation regarding a religious issue] saying that Muslims must kill Americans, whether military or civilian, and take their money. The *fatwa* said that this is compulsory for all Muslims all over the world who are capable of doing so. This marked a very important change in Zawahiri's philosophy. This *fatwa* shifted the battle from one targeting the near enemy to one targeting the far enemy, namely the United States and Israel. There were some indications in Zawahiri's writings in 1997 that made analysts believe that he was undergoing a change of philosophy marked by changes in his approach. He started showing more interest in the Palestinian cause and the Arab–Israeli conflict in general. In 1997, he wrote an article in the Egyptian Islamic Jihad bulletin entitled "America and the Issue of *Jihad* on Jews in Cairo." In this article, he mentioned the annual report issued by the American State Department about Islamist activities and leaders, which coincided with the issuance of the verdict of the military court that heard the Khān al-Khalili case. This article was the first indication in the dialogue of Zawahiri and Islamic Jihad of the new anti-American philosophy. In November 1997, he wrote another article entitled, "America and the Illusion of Power," in which he said that it is possible to administer blows to the Americans despite their strength. The change was even more clear in his article entitled, "Muslim *Umma*, Unite in Your *Jihad* on America," which unequivocally instigated Muslims to hit American targets.

Reasons for the changes in Zawahiri's approach

1. All the armed operations that targeted top-ranking government officials were foiled. For example, Nazeeh Nosihi Rasheed and Dia'

al-Deen implemented a suicide operation with the aim of assassinating former interior minister Hassan al-Alfi. Both assassins were killed in the attack, but al-Alfi survived. Also the group failed in the assassination attempt on former prime minister 'Atef Sidqi, which was led by Al-Sayyid Salāh and a number of other members who came from Yemen to perform this operation. The operation resulted in the killing of a child named Shayma' who was injured by flying splinters from the car that they blew up in front of Sidqi's house. The death of Shayma' led to public furor against Islamic Jihad, akin to the anger caused by killing car shop owner Sayyid Yehia in Qaliubiyya (the only eyewitness in the assassination attempt on Sidqi). This operation only led to more public outrage against the group.

2. The number of arrests of group members was increasing. Several administrative errors led to the arrest of members inside Egypt. The numerous foiled operations were another factor that led to more arrests, especially of dormant members who were not on the watch lists of the security authorities. In October 1993, for instance, the authorities foiled an operation in which a member was trying to steal a truck in Imbāba to use to transport weapons and explosives that the group was planning to steal from a military unit. The attempt led to the killing of the driver and his assistant and the arrest of about 800 members. Notable among them was Magdi Sālem, who was at that time the leader of Islamic Jihad in Cairo. Other members that were not on the security authorities' watch lists in a number of governorates such as Alexandria, Sharqiyya and Beheira were also arrested. Engineer Solimān Nasr al-Deen was arrested in possession of a list of the names of the group's members in Egypt.

3. There was a general deterioration in the group in the period between late 1993 and 1995, partly because of the lack of financial resources for the group to finance its activities and the living expenses of its leaders and members, especially the ones in Yemen and Sudan. Zawahiri did not have the money to pay salaries to the leaders of the group. Orders were issued to a number of members of the group at the time to try to find financial resources. In a bid to find

financial resources for the group, some of its leading figures traveled to Albania to work for relief agencies there. A percentage of their salaries as relief workers went towards funding the group. This financial crisis caused some tension in the relationship between Zawahiri and his ally Osāma bin Lāden. Bin Lāden did not abide by his promises to provide all the financial resources the group and its members abroad needed. A trustworthy member of Islamic Jihad who was close to the decision-making process told me then that Zawahiri referred to bin Lāden in an article, published in the *Kalimat Haqq* [*A Word of Truth*] bulletin, when he wrote, "The young people sacrificed their lives, while the rich were sparing with their money." Ahmed al-Naggār told heartbreaking stories of the state of Islamic Jihad members during their stay in Yemen and Sudan and how they did not have enough money to survive. Many of them had to look for jobs, until Osāma bin Lāden struck a deal with the Taliban. This deal allowed bin Lāden to bring Islamic Jihad members to Afghanistan and pay $100 a month to each family.

4. Another reason that led to this change in Zawahiri's philosophy was the extradition of a number of leading figures from outside Egypt. For example, Albania extradited Ahmed Ibrahim al-Naggār, Shawqi Salāma Mostafa and Mohamed Hassan, while Bulgaria extradited 'Esām 'Abdel Tawwāb. The Egyptian police also arrested hundreds of members inside Egypt. Later, 108 members were tried before a military court in the Returnees from Albania case.

5. One of the biggest blows that affected the group and Zawahiri deeply was the arrest of Ahmed Salāma Mabrūk, one of Zawahiri's most prominent aides. Mabrūk was arrested in Azerbaijan along with Mohamed Sa'eed al-'Ashri, also known as Abu Khāled, and 'Esām Mohamed Hāfez Marzūq, who had Canadian citizenship. They were all extradited to Egypt. The police also seized a computer carried by Mabrūk, containing the names of group members all over the world. The computer revealed to the authorities the locations of group members living overseas, including new members that were not known to the Egyptian authorities, as well as some information about Al-Qaeda members. The seized computer had some information about a number of new members that Zawahiri had

managed to recruit abroad, such as Mohamed 'Atef, also known as Abu Hafs. 'Atef's real name was Sobhi 'Abdel 'Azeez Abu Senna. He was killed in the American bombardment of Kabul in November 2001. The military court issued very harsh sentences against the leaders of the group. An informed member told me that Mabrūk had disagreed with the deteriorating policies of the group and had cut himself off from any contact with Zawahiri until he was arrested in Azerbaijan.

It is important to see what Ahmed al-Naggār says about this period because he was directly affected by it. In his confessions in the Returnees from Albania case, Naggār said:

Since I left Egypt, I have noticed that when the group was trying to revive its activities in Egypt in 1992, it incurred serious losses in personnel, as the members of the Vanguards of Conquest were arrested. This led to the waste of a lot of resources, but the remaining members were still capable of administering strong blows to the Egyptian regime. Financial resources were decreasing, which coincided with the arrest of a big number of members in the 'Atef Sidqi case and increased losses in personnel, both of which resulted from the negligence of some members in terms of the security arrangements of the group. At the end of 1994, Zawahiri thought of attacking the Egyptian Embassy in Islamabad, and Khān al-Khalili on the same day. He was thinking of implementing these two operations, and then taking a break from military operations for a while to reorganize the group.

6. Internal divisions were another important factor. I have pointed out earlier that Zawahiri managed in the period between 1987 and 1990 to regroup the members that subscribe ideologically to the *jihādi* approach and to gather them under one banner by establishing Islamic Jihad. The breaking away of some members was a main factor leading to the weakening of the group. It eventually forced Zawahiri to stop armed operations in Egypt and sign an agreement to join the International Islamic Front for Jihad on the Jews and Crusaders with Osāma bin Lāden. One of the members that

disagreed with Zawahiri was Ahmed Hussein 'Ogayza, who is an old member from the group from Beni Suef.[4] 'Ogayza was one of the main intellectuals of the group, and he participated in setting out its policies. He broke away due to disagreements with Zawahiri when he was in Afghanistan in 1993. He also convinced other members to leave the group with him, including 'Esām 'Abdel Tawwāb. The disagreements with 'Ogayza led to the formation of the Vanguards of Conquest. This was a crisis that weakened the group, which was one of the reasons why I disagreed with those who broke away from Zawahiri. I announced at the time that the Vanguards of Conquest was not a separate group, and that Islamic Jihad and the Vanguards of Conquest were two names for the same group led by Zawahiri. This was clear from the fact that the four accused in the Vanguards of Conquest cases that were tried by a military court were shouting their allegiance to Zawahiri from behind bars.

Another problem that weakened the group was the breaking away of its greatest intellectual, Dr. Sayyid Imām 'Abdel 'Azeez, also known as Fadl, who led it at a very critical time in its early days. 'Abdel 'Azeez is the writer of *The Basis for Preparedness*, which is considered the group's constitution, containing its intellectual and jurisprudential philosophy. After his decision to leave the group, no member produced *shari'a* studies on the level of the work of 'Abdel 'Azeez.

7. Sheikh Osāma bin Lāden was an important factor in the changing of Zawahiri's approach. Zawahiri managed to introduce drastic changes to Osāma bin Lāden's philosophy after they first met in Afghanistan in the middle of 1986, mainly because of the friendship that developed between them. Zawahiri convinced bin Lāden of his *jihādi* approach, turning him from a fundamentalist preacher whose main concern was relief work, into a *jihādi* fighter, clashing with despots and American troops in the Arab world. Zawahiri gave bin Lāden some of his closest confidants to help him. They later became the main figures in bin Lāden's Al-Qaeda. These confidants include 'Ali al-Rasheedi, an ex-municipal policeman in Egypt who was fired following Sadāt's assassination in October 1981

because of his religious activities. 'Ali al-Rasheedi was known in Afghanistan as Abu 'Ubayda al-Bansheeri. Another top aide of Zawahiri's that he assigned to help bin Lāden was Sobhi 'Abdel 'Azeez Abu Senna, known as Abu Hafs and Mohamed 'Atef. He was born in the Beheira governorate. He was expelled from his military service because of his religious orientations. Then he left Egypt to perform jihad in Afghanistan early on in the Afghan war against the Soviets. Al-Bansheery and Abu Hafs on the other hand did not belong to any Islamist group before they went to Afghanistan to fight the Soviets, but Zawahiri succeeded in recruiting them there. Some people wrongly believe that Osāma bin Lāden took a *jihādi* approach due to the influence of Sheikh 'Abdullah 'Azzām, the leader of Arab *mujāhideen* in Afghanistan. 'Azzām used bin Lāden's financial help to provide relief services to the *mujāhideen* in their war against the Soviets. The impact that 'Azzām had on bin Lāden was limited to political and geographical issues related to jihad against the Soviets. 'Azzām was not interested in clashing with the Arab governments that supported him. Still, 'Azzām's interaction with bin Lāden laid the groundwork for Zawahiri's influence.

Not only did Zawahiri influence bin Lāden, the latter impacted the philosophy of Zawahiri and of Islamic Jihad. For example, bin Lāden advised Zawahiri to stop armed operations in Egypt and to ally with him against their common enemies: the United States and Israel. His advice to Zawahiri came upon their return to Afghanistan, when bin Lāden ensured the safety of Zawahiri and the Islamic Jihad members under the banner of the Taliban, who at that time controlled 95 per cent of the country.

Ahmed al-Naggār, in his confessions in the Returnees from Albania case, said, "The Taliban movement made it conditional on Osāma bin Lāden to be directly responsible for the Arab Afghans." It was natural for bin Lāden to lead the International Islamic Front for Jihad on the Jews and Crusaders. He excelled at stirring the feelings of Arabs and Muslims when speaking on the Palestinian cause and when threatening the American presence in the Gulf. He argued that the Jewish lobby that controls the United States weakens the Muslim position. The main mission of the

Front was to rid Arab and Muslim lands of American hegemony. Zawahiri accepted bin Lāden's offer to form the Front, which was established in February 1998. His acceptance was due to the administrative problems that Islamic Jihad suffered, and its lack of financial resources. While bin Lāden was the leader of the Front, Zawahiri was clearly the main architect, along with other Egyptian Islamic Jihad members such as Abu Hafs, Sayf al-'Adl, Nasr Fahmi also known as Mohamed Salāh, Tāriq Anwar Sayyid Ahmed and Tharwat Salāh Shehāta.

Zawahiri's alliance with Osāma bin Lāden changed his philosophy from one prioritizing combat with the near enemy to one of confronting the far enemy: the United States and Israel. This development caused some confusion to Islamic Jihad members. Many were reluctant at first, but eventually agreed to be part of the Front in order to benefit from the many advantages it offered. As Naggār put it, no members could refuse to join the Front, except for the asylum seekers in European countries. Anyone who refused to join the Front would find himself alone with only his own resources and contacts.

8. Zawahiri was impacted by the Gamā'a al-Islāmiyya initiative to stop all armed operations inside and outside of Egypt. He opposed the idea of nonviolent Islamic activism through his frequent comments against the Muslim Brotherhood, which culminated in his book, *Al-Hasād al-Murr* [*The Bitter Harvest*], which was dedicated to criticizing the nonviolent approach of the group.

In 1996, Khāled Ibrahim, the leader of the Gamā'a al-Islāmiyya in Aswan, called for ceasing all armed operations for a year, a move which I supported. Zawahiri, on the other hand, issued a statement in response to Ibrahim's call, which included his reasons for refusing to stop armed operations. When the rest of the leaders of the Gamā'a al-Islāmiyya, including the most prominent figures, called for a ceasefire in July, 1997, Zawahiri found himself in a quandary. He only ordered his group to launch armed operations against top government figures in 1993 in order to keep up with the Gamā'a al-Islāmiyya, which was launching similar operations, and to win some of the popularity that the Gamā'a al-Islāmiyya enjoyed among young people.

Because the Gamā'a al-Islāmiyya boasted a larger membership, and because it had initiated the armed struggle against the Egyptian government, the decision of its sheikhs to stop armed operations and seek a peaceful approach made it difficult for others to break this ceasefire. By that time, Zawahiri had already been considering stopping the armed operations of Islamic Jihad in Egypt, but his reasons were different from those of the Gamā'a al-Islāmiyya. Where the main reason for the decision of the Gamā'a al-Islāmiyya was the heightened interest in the question of Palestine, Zawahiri wanted to stop operations because of the weak points that were expanding in his group. Unlike Islamic Jihad, the Gamā'a al-Islāmiyya did not suffer from internal divisions among members. It was also bigger with more preachers, cadres and leaders.

Zawahiri had intended to stop his operations when the Gamā'a al-Islāmiyya's operations were at full throttle in order to keep the reasons for his decision secret. He did not want people to know that it was the weaknesses in his group that were forcing Islamic Jihad to cut back its activities. The ceasefire initiative of the sheikhs of the Gamā'a al-Islāmiyya gained great popularity among all *jihādi* Islamists, even those close to Zawahiri. Still, out of loyalty, they could do nothing but criticize the initiative in their statements. Under pressure from the Gamā'a al-Islāmiyya initiative, Zawahiri decided to join the International Islamic Front for Jihad on the Jews and Crusaders. For him, it was a good channel through which to continue his activities, and a way to redesign the organizational structure of Islamic Jihad. It was after this collaboration that a new Zawahiri emerged: one more interested in the liberation of Palestine, urging Muslims to launch armed operations against the United States and Israel.

Zawahiri's change of approach towards the liberation of Palestine and enmity to the United States was not in line with his conviction that the near enemy, the Egyptian regime, should be fought first. The ceasefire decision of the Gamā'a al-Islāmiyya, on the other hand, was in accordance with the group's original peaceful philosophy, which appeared with the group's inception in the 1970s.

Changes in Zawahiri's Ideology

Zawahiri charged some of the members of his group with preparing and executing the bombing of the two American embassies in Nairobi and Darussalam. He wanted people to know of his connection to the operation, which is why he issued a statement on August 4, 1998:

This is a statement from Egyptian Islamic Jihad about the extradition of three of our brothers in certain Eastern European countries. The first brother is Tāriq, who was arrested in an Eastern European country that is known for hating Muslims, while he was there with his Albanian wife. Less than two months after this crime, Abu Islām and Abu Mahmūd as well as two other brothers were arrested in Albania. They were accused of being members of a group that has declared jihad on America and Israel and their agents, as well as cooperating with the *mujāhideen* in Kosovo, outside American control. We would like to tell the Americans that their message has arrived and that the response is being prepared. The Americans should read it carefully because we will write it, God willing, in the language they understand.

Through this statement which he issued a few hours before the bombing of the two embassies in Nairobi and Darussalam, Zawahiri wanted to tell the world that he took part in the operation, not because of the reasons that he mentioned, but because he wanted to gain popular support from Arabs and Muslims by combating the American aggression. He needed this popularity after the failure of his operations in Egypt, in which he did not target Jews or Americans, but rather ended up killing Egyptian civilians such as Sayyid Yehia and the child Shayma'. A statement issued by the Islamic Army for the Liberation of the Holy Places, which is affiliated with the Front, did not mention the reasons that Zawahiri declared for the bombing.

5

The Ceasefire Initiative of the Gamā'a al-Islāmiyya

The ceasefire initiative of the Gamā'a al-Islāmiyya was spearheaded by the historic leaders of the group, or those who are now serving prison sentences for involvement in the assassination of Sadāt. It caused widespread reaction either for or against it, and questions about its credibility among people who do not trust Islamists.

The most severe critic of the initiative was Zawahiri. There is a code of conduct among Islamist groups, which holds that no one should interfere in the internal affairs of any group other than their own. Zawahiri violated this code not only by criticizing the initiative, but also by launching an acute attack on all the people that had anything to do with it. At a later stage, he turned people against it. He even tried to hit the group from inside by urging those members of the Gamā'a al-Islāmiyya who opposed the initiative to go against their brothers in the group. He tried to convince Refā'i Ahmed Tāha, the head of the *shura* council[1] for the group, who was one of the main opponents of the initiative, to appear in public next to him and Osāma bin Lāden. He was hoping to send a message to Western and American media that Tāha was with bin Lāden and Zawahiri in their jihad on Israel and the United States. In fact, despite his opposition to the initiative, targeting Americans and their interests was never a priority for Tāha any more than it was for the historic leaders of the Gamā'a al-Islāmiyya in prison and other members living abroad. The curious thing is that Zawahiri never commented on the idea of mediation that some scholars and Islamic activists called for between the Islamic groups and the government in 1993.

I never tried to hide the role I played in any previous peaceful initiative and Zawahiri and his aides have an archive with everything that is published about the Islamic movement. In 1993, I wrote in support of another peaceful initiative that happened that year and led to the sacking of the then minister of the interior Mohamed 'Abdel Haleem Mūssa. I also supported the April 1996 initiative called for by Khāled Ibrahim.

My role in promoting the July 5, 1997 initiative of the Gamā'a al-Islāmiyya was different from my role in any of those previous initiatives. It began only after Mohamed al-Ameen 'Abdel 'Aleem read a statement prepared by the historic leaders of the Gamā'a al-Islāmiyya in a military court that was trying some of the members of the group, and ended soon after the *shura* council of the group issued its historic decision in March 1999 to end all armed operations inside and outside Egypt. At that point I decided that there was no longer any reason for me to talk about the peaceful approach as a strategic option for the Gamā'a al-Islāmiyya. My temporary role was necessary during the absence of many leaders of the group. When Hamdi 'Abdel Rahmān, one of the members who called for the peaceful solution, was released in early 2001, I felt that he could take over.

I first discussed my activities in the ceasefire initiatives with Zawahiri on a trip to London in March 1997 that I took with the purpose of delivering some lectures on human rights in Islam in a number of Islamic centers. I was received at the airport by 'Adil 'Abdel Mageed, head of the Maqreezy Center for Historical Studies (the Americans are currently attempting to extradite him to be tried for his connections with Osāma bin Lāden), along with Hani al-Sibā'i and Sheikh Mohamed al-Moqre'i, head of the Islamic Koran and *Sunna* Association. Both 'Abdel Mageed and Sibā'i used to work with me in a legal services office in downtown Cairo. Moqre'i is a well-known Gamā'a al-Islāmiyya preacher. They insisted on hosting me. As soon as I arrived at 'Adel 'Abdel Mageed's house, Zawahiri called me. After he congratulated me on arriving in London safely, he asked me, "Why are you making your brothers angry?" He reproached me mildly for my role in promoting Khāled Ibrahim's call for ceasefire in 1996 and told me that it had angered many brothers.

For a long time afterwards, I would discuss with Zawahiri by cellular phone the reasons for my support for efforts to stop armed operations in Egypt. The reasons that I enumerated to him differed little from the reasons that I told the press. I argued for an end to the bloodshed, and that the ceasefire is acceptable in Islamic *shari'a* in the case of weakness. I added that many innocent young people who had not committed any crime were in prison, and that thousands of families were suffering from poverty and other social problems because of the continued detention of their relatives. Zawahiri said that by my support of the initiative I had let the *mujāhideen* down. I told him that I prefer the peaceful *da'wa* way, and that a peaceful strategy does not necessarily imply more lenient goals. I argued for calling for Islam and telling the truth without fearing anyone or worrying about the consequences, including persecution. I added that jihad does not have to be restricted to the armed approach.

Zawahiri was not convinced by my argument, nor was I by his. However, we reached an agreement that each one of us should understand the other's viewpoint and that both of us are good Muslims who do not compromise our Islamic principles. During this phone conversation, Zawahiri tried to convince me to stay in London and to bring my family to stay with me there. He promised to help me get a permanent residence as an asylum seeker. He thought that my presence in London would be useful for Islamic Jihad. I politely rejected his offer and came back to Cairo.

It was a few months later that I announced the Gamā'a al-Islāmiyya initiative. The prominent leaders of the Gamā'a al-Islāmiyya delegated me to promote the initiative and verify to their brothers inside and outside Egypt that it was truly issued by them. I agreed to do so although I did not, and still do not belong to the group. I promoted the initiative according to what the sheikhs of the Gamā'a al-Islāmiyya asked me to do, without mentioning anything about Islamic Jihad or its leader Zawahiri. The imprisoned leaders of the Gamā'a al-Islāmiyya sent me a paper from the Tora Prison, handwritten by one of them, informing me of what I could announce if we lost contact with each other.

The paper included the following instructions among others:

1. Confirmation of the fact that armed operations did not start until *da'wa* and the activities of mosques were prohibited.
2. Statement that the state should not punish citizens for their beliefs.
3. Explanation of the issue of Christians. This had two components: First, churches are unrestricted in what they preach, but any Muslim who wants to deliver a sermon is required to get a permit from the authorities. Second, the Gamā'a al-Islāmiyya did not kill Christians because of their religious beliefs, but for other reasons.

In their paper to me, the leaders of the Gamā'a al-Islāmiyya asked me to concentrate on two points regarding the future of the group and the role it can play:

1. There should be an outlet for Islamic groups through a political and *da'wa* entity that calls people to Islam and fights external powers and their destructive ideas.
2. Islamic groups should be granted all the freedoms and rights to which they are entitled according to the Egyptian constitution. This would eliminate any reason for taking arms.

Some members of Islamic Jihad wanted to launch similar initiatives and tried to convince me to promote for them in the same way I promoted the Gamā'a al-Islāmiyya initiative. For instance, Nabeel al-Maghrebi and Ahmed Yusef Hamdullah called for ceasefire. I refused to use their statements and messages, because I knew this would have completely isolated Zawahiri.

I also refused the initiative voiced by Osāma Sedeeq Ayūb, an Islamic Jihad member who had previously broken away from Zawahiri. He had remained loyal to Islamic Jihad, and eventually joined Zawahiri again. Ayūb called for a ceasefire initiative from Germany, where he had sought asylum.

Hishām Abāza, one of the prominent leaders of Islamic Jihad in the Sharqiyya governorate, sent me a similar request while he was in prison. He wanted me to communicate some points with the "hajj,"[2] meaning Zawahiri. He advocated reaching reconciliation with the government based on:

- following a sound *da'wa* approach avoiding provocation of the authorities;
- establishing a system for dealing with Christians, as well as teaching people to consider them a part of us, which should therefore not be harmed;
- considering this reconciliation a request presented from the relatives of the detained members to the person in charge.

He also wrote that this initiative was not to hold unless "the man," meaning Zawahiri, agreed to it.

I advised Abāza to wait because I realized that his initiative would be fruitless, but he went ahead without getting Zawahiri's approval. He read the statement himself in the military court that was trying the accused in the Returnees from Albania case. In the end, no one took note of his initiative because it was not well prepared.

Even before Abāza's initiative, Mohamed Nasr Eddeen al-Ghazlāni, one of the leaders of the group in Giza, wanted me to adopt his initiative when he was being tried in 1998 in the Khān al-Khalili case. I told him that I could not promote his initiative despite our close friendship and my support for his call, which also coincided with that of the Gamā'a al-Islāmiyya. My philosophy was that because Zawahiri, the leader of Islamic Jihad, did not support the peaceful approach, representing Ghazlāni would amount to interference in the internal affairs of his group. I was surprised when, in one of the sessions of the military court that was looking into the Khān al-Khalili case, Ghazlāni read the following:

I agree with all that my esteemed teacher Montasser al-Zayyāt said before the honorable court in the session held on September 22, 1997, and I pray to God Almighty that he and the sincere group that work with him will be successful in their efforts to put out the fire of civil strife between the state and some of its citizens, kindled by the enemies of this nation. International Zionism, the most active of the three conspirators against our Muslim and Arab nation, is behind this civil strife in Egypt. There are malignant Zionist hands behind any destruction that happens. These hands are lighting and fueling the fire of civil strife.

Ghazlāni addressed the court chief judge saying:

Dear Sir, although the Jews are officially at peace with Egypt, their enmity towards the country has never died. The Jews want to ruin Egypt's present and future by targeting its young people because they are the secret of its strength, and because young people are the core of any civilization and advancement.

Then Ghazlāni mentioned three armed operations in which he could clearly see Jewish hands.

The first is the bombing of the Wadi al-Neel coffee shop, followed by the explosion of the Haram Tunnel and the assassination attempt on Dr. 'Omar 'Abdel 'Azeez, a professor at Al-Azhar University, when his car was blown up in the Qolaly.

He added that 'Abdel 'Azeez accused the Jews in the investigations of trying to kill him, explaining that they wanted to cause civil strife among Egyptian young people.
He stated:

The Jews will benefit from civil strife in Egypt because this will assure that Egyptian officials are too busy with their internal affairs to notice the Jews' conspiracies and expansionist schemes. The Jews also exaggerated what happened to tourists to give the impression that Egypt is not a safe tourist destination, thus turning thousands of dollars away to other countries, and weakening the Egyptian economy. They want a Mediterranean market in which Zionism controls the markets of the whole region.

He continued:

Dear Sir, I hope from the bottom of my heart that the efforts exerted by Montasser al-Zayyāt and other sincere people from our beloved

Egypt will be successful and I hope that these efforts will help unite our nation to face up to the grave dangers besetting us and our Arab and Muslim nation from all directions.

Ghazlāni was sentenced to 15 years of hard labor.

The above are only a sample of the messages that I received from leading Islamic Jihad figures, despite Zawahiri's claims that no one from his group was involved in this initiative. At the time, I did not use these messages in rebutting Zawahiri's claims that all those that called for ceasefire were from the Gamā'a al-Islāmiyya, and were forced into it, nor his accusations and declarations in which he criticized the Gamā'a al-Islāmiyya initiative and me personally.

Zawahiri's book *Knights Under the Banner of the Prophet* included considerable criticism of the ceasefire initiative; however he did not make any references to the members of his group who supported it. Instead his criticism was directed towards me, and centered on two points:

1. He wrote that I have been trying to promote the idea of undermining jihad against the government and its American and Jewish allies inside and outside Egypt. He added that I have been making contacts about this issue since 'Abdel Haleem Mūssa, the former minister of the interior, was in office.

2. He criticized what he saw as privileges accruing to me, that he said many ministers in Egypt do not enjoy. He pointed out that I can secure a visit to any prison in Egypt on the same day that I request it, and that I have been known to hold meetings with the most important leaders that oppose the government. He went on to say that I have succeeded in passing messages from outside Egypt to these leaders and in passing their statements to the press. He declared that I was delegated by the historic leaders and that I have become their mouthpiece. He added that I have satellite and radio interviews as their delegate because I am the only connection between them in their prisons and the outside world, and that any messages that they send out come through me.

Zawahiri implied that I was motivated by reasons other than a genuine belief in the peaceful approach by pointing out threats leveled at me from the authorities. He wrote:

A new dimension to the initiative becomes clear when you add to this the fact that State Security officers had told Zayyāt, before releasing him after the Bar Association sit-in in 1994, that if he crossed the red line, he would only cost them a few piasters, the price of a bullet.

He continued, "Zayyāt's efforts enjoy the support of the imprisoned leaders of the Gamā'a al-Islāmiyya, who have delegated him and repeated their support for him on several occasions."

Zawahiri tried in different parts of his book to drive a wedge between the leaders of the Gamā'a al-Islāmiyya and me. He described the initiative as having been "forced on them," and implied that I had also been forced into my stance. He forgot, perhaps deliberately, that the imprisoned Gamā'a al-Islāmiyya leaders are not easily coerced into anything that is against their beliefs. They have always had great courage in expressing their opinions and bearing the consequences both in times of war and in times of peace.

These leaders clearly expressed their anti-government beliefs before the State Security Court. They even submitted their religious research and beliefs to the court. Their provocation of the hangman reached its highest when they arrived in red uniforms to the session when the verdict was scheduled to be pronounced. This was meant as a sign that they were eager to die. They have never bowed for a promise or a gift and they have learnt from the experiences of their predecessors that such promises are never kept. They did not propose their ceasefire initiative until they had already spent 17 years in prison, meaning that the period they had already served was much more than the period that they might avoid by compromising their principles. Finally, these leaders also have many channels of communication outside of Egypt, through the many leaders who live abroad and still pledge allegiance to them. These members abroad were studying the situation and verifying the same information through many sources, without fear of the authorities.

Zawahiri contradicted himself several times when he addressed my role in the ceasefire initiative. For example, he mentioned that my promotion of the initiative was forced on me, citing the incident when the State Security officers threatened to liquidate me if I overstepped the red line. At the same time, he related that I had been convinced that ceasefire was a good idea as early as 1993, when some scholars wanted to mediate between the Islamic groups and the former minister of the interior Mohamed 'Abdel Haleem Mūssa.

I understand the difficult conditions that Zawahiri suffered and the cruel circumstances that must have pushed him to write this, including living in mountains and caves in an atmosphere of war and fighting. What Zawahiri wrote did not change my love and respect for him, and this is why I have accepted his criticism. I am sure I will forgive him before God on the Day of Judgment, the Day of Resurrection, when money and offspring are not useful anymore. I hope that both of us will be like the people that God mentioned in the Koran: "And we shall remove from their breasts any deep feeling of bitterness [that they might have]. [So they will be like] brothers facing each other on thrones."[3] Despite the love I have for Zawahiri, honesty requires that I reveal all the facts without any distortion, even if in doing so I reveal him as rash or wrong.

Zawahiri forgot that the initiative, the promotion of which was entrusted to me, was the choice of the Gamā'a al-Islāmiyya and that it coincided with my own beliefs. He did not mention many of my announcements about the initiative. I have repeatedly said:

I was as surprised as were the others when Mohamed al-Ameen 'Abdel 'Aleem read the initiative during the military court session on July 5, 1997, where I was sitting with other lawyers waiting to perform our role in defending the accused. I took no part in its formulation.

I am saying this not to prove my innocence, but because it is the truth.

Zawahiri was unjust in claiming that all my writings call for facing up to the normalization of relations with Israel. My membership in a number of anti-normalization centers refutes his claim. He fails to see that the main objective of the April 1996 ceasefire initiative and of the July 1997 ceasefire was to pool our efforts and energies to perform jihad against the Jews and to liberate Palestine, including Jerusalem, from the Zionists.

He was also wrong in claiming that I called for stopping jihad against the Jews. There were a large number of Islamic movement activists whose opinions in the interpretation of jihad differed considerably from that of Zawahiri. Jihad against the Jews, the enemies of the *umma*, requires preparation and patience in securing the means to ensure a victory. It will not be achieved through harming the United States. This jihad requires us to inform the *umma* of the dangers of cultural, intellectual and ideological normalization with the Zionist entity. We must explain to all segments of society the real battle: the economic one, which includes boycotting Israeli and American products and providing the necessary support to the Palestinian people, until the right time for the military battle comes. When it is the right time for military action, the whole united *umma* will take part to gain the victory of which the Prophet, may peace and prayers of God be upon him, spoke.

Neither in the statements of the Gamā'a al-Islāmiyya leaders, nor in my own writing have I ever advocated forsaking our strategic objective of instituting Islamic *shari'a* in letter and spirit, nor have I accepted anything that is not in line with these objectives. We never accepted any other law than Islamic *shari'a*, and we never promoted ideas that contradict it. Our ideas contradict only Zawahiri's philosophy.

Zawahiri's claim that I was the only channel of communication between the Gamā'a al-Islāmiyya leaders in Egypt and their brothers abroad is not true. If it were, I would have been proud to have admitted to such an honor. The fact is that there were many prominent fellow Islamist lawyers who paid similar visits to the imprisoned leaders and passed on their statements. Some of them even went to visit them in the Tora Prison at the request of members of the group abroad to hear their reasons for launching the initiative and to verify the information that I announced. I only made a few visits in three years and I have not been able to make any visits for the last year. I always made sure that my permits to visit them came from the Public Prosecutor's office. It is true that the aim behind these visits facilitated the issuance of permits, which would have otherwise been difficult to obtain. However there are many young Islamist lawyers who continue to visit the Gamā'a al-Islāmiyya leaders in the Tora Prison, and with greater ease than I enjoy.

My relationship with the authorities was not close, and I could have made many complaints about their violations against me. I could have decided to completely cut off all links with them. Indeed, this would have improved my image in the circles of Islamic groups.

Many lawyers entered the arena of Islamist activity through their jobs, and followed in the footsteps of the leaders of Islamist groups to gain certain privileges with them, only to renounce their allegiance to the Islamist movement when it ceased to serve their interests. I did not enter the arena of Islamist activity through my job as a lawyer. I am a loyal son of the modern Islamic awakening. I have been under its banner since my youth. When first I decided to stop my organizational activities, Zawahiri accepted my decision, recognizing that I was not qualified to play a clandestine organizational role after having been tried in the Jihad case. Many of those released from prison under similar circumstances ceased any Islamic activities, and took completely different routes. I maintain that I continue to defend my identity and Islamic faith, but through other means. This defense involves the same dangers as clandestine organizational work does. Now, 20 years later, Zawahiri has taken to criticizing me for this choice.

Zawahiri was not critical of any of my fellow lawyers who also expressed their support to the Gamā'a al-Islāmiyya initiative by releasing announcements of the imprisoned Islamic Jihad members. In 1997, in an interview with the AFP that took place before they made these announcements, he said that no one from his group was part of the initiative. Even after it became clear that this was false, he chose not to comment on these initiative supporters in his book, *Knights Under the Banner of the Prophet*.

Although I bore the brunt of Zawahiri's criticism, he also criticized the initiative itself as an approach. In *Knights Under the Banner of the Prophet* (on page 255), he wrote that it shook the clear vision of the group. This vision focused on ousting the Egyptian regime which befriends the enemies of Islam (the Jews and the Americans) and does not rule according to Islamic *shari'a*. He was also critical of Osāma Rushdi, a prominent leader in the Gamā'a al-Islāmiyya who sought asylum in Holland. He said of Rushdi that he "talked about the initiative when he disowned the Luxor incident, which took place on November 17, 1997. He mentioned it again when he was talking to Refā'i Tāha in the same context." Zawahiri touched on Rushdy's opinion regarding why Sheikh 'Omar 'Abdel Rahmān decided to withdraw his support for the initiative. Rushdi summarized the situation:

> The Sheikh ('Abdel Rahmān) reached this conclusion when he learnt that thousands of members were still being detained and tortured. Perhaps the lack of communication between him and the members, his family and lawyers in Egypt led to the distortion of the information that he received about the situation in Egypt and the opinions of other leading figures in the Gamā'a al-Islāmiyya.

Zawahiri's comment on Rushdi's explanation was:

> Rushdi pretended to forget the enmity the Egyptian government displayed toward the Sheikh, and its aggression against him. He also pretended to forget that the nature of this enmity is ideological. Then he suggested bargaining for the release of the Sheikh on the terms that he cease to be a source of disturbance to the government. He said that the Sheikh would also support peace and relieve the tension, not only in Egypt but also on the international level, in support of the unanimous agreement of the group.

In his book, Zawahiri compared previous Gamā'a al-Islāmiyya stances to Rushdi's proposal for the release of Sheikh 'Omar 'Abdel Rahmān. "What happened during these years? Are their basic beliefs still the same?" Zawahiri wondered. He concluded that Rushdi's announcements are not a simple change in his beliefs, but a coup against the group.

Rushdi emailed me the following response to Zawahiri's criticism:

I find it hard to write a rebuttal of the severe criticism of me and of the Gamā'a al-Islāmiyya that Zawahiri wrote in his book *Knights Under the Banner of the Prophet* following the ceasefire initiative. What makes it harder to write a rebuttal is that Dr. Zawahiri is going through a hard time since some members of his family were martyred, may God have mercy upon them. I am writing this as a reply to what he wrote because I have been following the unfolding of events and have participated in bringing some of them about. What I am writing should not be considered an expression of the stance of the Gamā'a al-Islāmiyya, as I am not delegated to speak on its behalf.

I met Zawahiri in the Tora Prison, where we stayed in the same cell for about three years. He was the picture of humbleness and politeness. He never expressed disagreement with any of the members of the Gamā'a al-Islāmiyya, who were the biggest group in prison, probably because of his shyness. Zawahiri changed so much when he went to Peshawar. There, he was influenced by others in an atmosphere that was characterized by hardline policies. He formed a new group in 1987 called *Tanzeem al-Jihād* [Jihad Organization], a year later he changed it to its current name, Islamic Jihad. In order to set his group apart from other groups, he started criticizing the intellectual and religious approach of the Gamā'a al-Islāmiyya, as well as its prominent figures, whenever there was a chance to do so. This way, he thought he could recruit more members to his newly born group.

In 1991, Zawahiri published a small book, in which he said that a blind person should not be the *ameer*.[4] He distributed many copies of it in Peshawar, Pakistan and many other countries. In the book, he said that in books of Islamic *shari'a*, there are a number of conditions that have to be met in any Great Imām,[5] including having sound senses. What a strange analogy! Through this book, he was saying that the fact that Sheikh 'Omar 'Abdel Rahmān is the *ameer* of the Gamā'a al-Islāmiyya is a violation of Islamic *shari'a*. I remember one time after we performed the Friday prayers in 1990, we talked about a picture of the late Dr. 'Alā' Mohiyee al-Deen in a newspaper. There was a poster behind him saying, "We welcome equal dialogue." Zawahiri asked one of the people there to fetch him a copy. He was speaking angrily and making a big issue out of the whole thing, and claiming that this was a change in the group philosophy, among other accusations against the initiative. The dialogue mentioned in the poster was with *azhari* scholars at the latter's request, which was not a new policy. There were many public dialogues in a number of governorates. This did not mean that the group had given up any of its principles. There is nothing wrong with these dialogues.

He accused me of the same things that he mentioned in his book because I spoke in one of these dialogues in Egypt in March of 1989. I was taken from prison along with a number of other detainees. We were supposed to go to court to look into our detention complaint, but we were surprised that they took us to the Islamic Studies Center instead. They had organized a dialogue with us there to make the then Minister of the interior Zaki Badr look good, especially after he had had a fight with Tal'at Raslan, a Wafd Party member at the People's Assembly, a few days before the dialogue meeting. The meeting included the late sheikhs Sha'rawy and Ghazāli, as well as the then Minister of *awqāf* [religious endowments] Mohamed 'Ali Mahgūb, whom I had met twice before that. The State Security officers, who were supposed to release us after this meeting, attended as well.

After the three sheikhs spoke, I was asked to speak. I said, "How can I speak when I have just come from prison where I have been tortured because of speaking?" When the Minister insisted, I said that there are young people and children in prison being tortured and that the officers tell them they have a *fatwa* from the three sheikhs Sha'rawy, Ghazāli and Mahgūb that they are permitted to do that. The officers were referring to the so-called Tripartite Statement, which the three sheikhs issued from the courtyard of the honored Al-Azhar Mosque, two months before the dialogue meeting. I added that some of the detained were children less than ten years of age.

They were arrested in the 'Ein Shams incidents of December 1988. These children were crying at night because the cells were dark. This is when Sheikh Ghazāli jumped to his feet to condemn torture, reciting God's words, "Verily, those who put into trial the believing men and believing women [by torturing them and burning them], and then do not turn in repentance [to God], then they will have the torment of Hell, and they will have the punishment of the burning Fire."[6] He then said that he never issued the *fatwa*, in question. Sheikh Sha'rawy also denied that he issued the *fatwa* saying that God will reward us for that.

I then talked about the statement the three sheikhs issued, and other accusations made against us. Namely, that we consider some people disbelievers. I told the sheikhs that they should have verified this by talking to us before making judgments, and explained that the accusation was based only on some distorted press claims. I added that we do not have a different understanding of Islam and that we follow the Koran and the *sunna* in the way the scholars of the old times understood them, with the same beliefs as any Sunni Muslim. I also pointed out that we do not consider anyone a disbeliever because he/she is sinful, unless they believe that the sin they commit is *halāl* [acceptable according to Islamic law]. Sheikh Sha'rawy answered, "Then we did not mean you." I replied, "But who else is in prison?"

These dialogues did not harm us, so why would it be a bad idea to get involved in them? On the contrary, they were very useful, correcting the distorted image that these sheikhs had of us. The dialogues were never published, despite the presence of all the state-owned newspapers and TV stations. They only broadcast my pictures on the news without voice and in the newspapers without mentioning any of the things I said. Following this meeting, Zaki Badr ordered that we should be kept away from similar dialogue seminars, after he noticed that they in fact serve our cause. He also made his famous announcement that he welcomes dialogue provided that it convinces us we are wrong.

Osāma Rushdi described the relationship between Zawahiri and the late Sheikh 'Abdullah 'Azzām by saying,

Even Sheikh 'Abdullah 'Azzām, the imām of the *mujāhideen*, was criticized by Zawahiri and by his brother. They accused him of being an agent for the Saudis one time and of the Americans another time, among other accusations. I still remember a heated discussion between Zawahiri and me when we ran into each other on the street in Peshawar, a couple of days before 'Azzām was assassinated. Zawahiri criticized the Gamā'a al-Islāmiyya for its good relationship with 'Azzām, and tried to convince me that 'Azzām was an agent. When the latter was assassinated along with his two sons, I met Zawahiri at the funeral, where he was praising the martyred sheikh. This is exactly what they did with Dr. 'Omar 'Abdel Rahmān when he was imprisoned! Then Zawahiri turned against the Muslim Brotherhood by publishing his book *The Bitter Harvest*. Zawahiri tried at that stage to demolish all the Islamic figures that were present at the time. He said that his group would be able to manage the struggle alone.

Then Osāma Rushdi talked about the front that Zawahiri established with Osāma bin Lāden.

While Zawahiri is critical in his book of the randomness of Islamic work, we notice that he made the decision to blow up the Egyptian Embassy in Islamabad in 1995 in a very random way. He says in his book *Knights Under the Banner of the Prophet*, "After performing a study, we decided to form a group to take revenge. The group was charged with hitting the American Embassy in Islamabad. If they could not do that, they would hit any American target in Pakistan. If they could not do that either, they would hit the embassy of a Western country that is known for its enmity to Muslims. If they could not do that, they would hit the Egyptian Embassy."

This is how policies are made and serious decisions are taken. This is how easy it is to target the interests of countries in four continents.

The formation of the International Islamic Front for Jihad on the Jews and Crusaders was equally random. When we asked Refā'i Tāha, may God help him, about the signing of the Front in 1998, he said that he was informed by telephone about the intention of the group to issue a statement expressing their support to the Iraqi people against the aggression that they were suffering. He agreed to the inclusion of his name in the statement. He was surprised to discover later that the statement referred to the establishment of a new front, and that it included a very serious *fatwa* that all Muslims would be required to follow. Tāha said, "All this happened without any clear approval from the Gamā'a al-Islāmiyya regarding participation in the Front. The Gamā'a al-Islāmiyya found itself a member of a front that they knew nothing about."

Refā'i Tāha goes on to say:

Dr. Ayman al-Zawahiri and the members of his group were not successful even in the simple operations they attempted in Egypt. They incurred a lot of losses because of the computer that was seized that contained the names and addresses of all the group members and its sympathizers in Egypt, which led to the arrest of more than 1,000 of them, most of whom were tried. This is why he decided to stop armed operations in Egypt even before the Gamā'a al-Islāmiyya announced its initiative. Still he denies his brothers in the Gamā'a al-Islāmiyya their right to announce what he had already decided. If Zawahiri refused this initiative, which was not his concern anyway, why did he not resume the operations of his own group?

Not only did Zawahiri try several times to drive a wedge between me and the imprisoned leaders of the Gamā'a al-Islāmiyya, he also tried to drive a wedge between me and Dr. 'Omar 'Abdel Rahmān, Refā'i Tāha and the leading figures of the Gamā'a al-Islāmiyya abroad. He not only criticized me but also made fun of my activities when he said:

In fact, Montasser al-Zayyāt does not only consider himself an authorized representative of the Gamā'a al-Islāmiyya, but also gives himself the right to announce that the declarations of Refā'i Tāha and 'Omar 'Abdel Rahmān do not necessarily represent the stance of the group.

Zawahiri twisted the facts by making this claim because he knows how highly respected Refā'i Tāha and 'Omar 'Abdel Rahmān are to the rest of the members of the group. He also said that I was an intruder who claimed to be its representative. He knows very well that I respect myself and that since I terminated my attachment to any group in 1984, I have not spoken on anyone's behalf. He knows that if I wrongly made such a claim, the group would have announced that I did not have anything to do with it, which was not the case. Zawahiri thought that by making such claims, the leading figures of the Gamā'a al-Islāmiyya would disown the initiative and declare that I had nothing to do with the whole issue. But he was not successful and will not be because the initiative is the decision of the Gamā'a al-Islāmiyya. Mostafa Hamza, a Gamā'a al-Islāmiyya member, told me several times that Zawahiri was putting pressure on the group to deny their relationship with me. But the leading figures of the group, whether its sheikhs who are captives in the Tora Prison or its leading figures abroad, including his close friend Refā'i Tāha, would not heed his requests. His book was merely an effort to sap the foundations of the ceasefire initiative before the public by questioning my relationship with the Gamā'a al-Islāmiyya.

My response to Zawahiri's claims

First, I have infinite respect for Dr. 'Omar 'Abdel Rahmān. To this day, we are close friends. The sheikh has expressed warm feelings towards me on several occasions. For example, when I was arrested in 1982, he worked to cure the wounds that resulted from this arrest. He is a very wise leader who knows how to treat his sons. When I was invited to a press conference following the declaration of the establishment of the International Islamic Front for Jihad on the Jews and Crusaders, I called for the establishment an international front for promoting Islam through peaceful means. I did not expect that my initiative, which occupied only a few lines in a long announcement, would capture the attention of 'Abdel Rahmān in his prison in the United States.

I was pleasantly surprised when he sent me a private message expressing his support for my initiative.

Second, during a press conference held in my office after the announcement that Dr. 'Omar 'Abdel Rahmān had withdrawn his support for the ceasefire initiative, I confirmed that he had not cancelled the initiative, but only suspended his support for it. He delegated the imprisoned historic leaders of the group to make a decision based on the realities of the situation. By taking this decision, Dr. 'Omar 'Abdel Rahmān proved that he was a judicious, far-sighted and flexible leader because if he had canceled the initiative, this would have caused the imprisoned leaders of the group great embarrassment and a great wound. They would have been forced to cancel it on their part. That is why I wanted to explain to people through the media that although Dr. 'Omar 'Abdel Rahmān had withdrawn his support, he left the initiative under assessment and study.

In his book *Knights Under the Banner of the Prophet*, Zawahiri attempted to call my intentions to question by mentioning that I hid part of 'Omar 'Abdel Rahmān's message from the press. What I did not mention in the press conference were matters related to his family and private issues about the imprisoned leaders of the Gamā'a al-Islāmiyya. These do not concern the public. The press conference was the result of a last minute decision, and was intended to defend a decision that some people were seeking to undermine, in the hope of returning to a state of tension. I believed that we needed to arrange our priorities and assess our performance carefully, and that continued tension would not have been good for us.

In calling the press conference, I did not transcend the people in charge, the leaders of the Gamā'a al-Islāmiyya. The information that was given there was clearly supported. For instance, as I said then, I had received a phone call from Mostafa Hamza. Zawahiri, may God forgive him, did not mention that.

Third, in his old statements and in his book *Knights Under the Banner of the Prophet*, in which he assessed the initiative, Zawahiri overlooked Dr. 'Omar 'Abdel Rahmān's wholehearted support for the July 5, 1997 initiative of the Gamā'a al-Islāmiyya. He overlooked the statements 'Abdel Rahmān himself issued, in the absence of external pressures, from his prison in the United States. Zawahiri omitted this information, realizing that to mention 'Abdel Rahmān's initial positive stance toward the initiative would have weakened all his criticisms.

Fourth, Zawahiri failed to mention a message that Dr. 'Omar 'Abdel Rahmān sent to his son 'Abdullah in which he confirmed that the initiative is still valid and charged my humble self to promote it. The London-based *Al-Hayat* newspaper published the message in its entirety.

Finally, I had a close and longstanding friendship with the Gamā'a al-Islāmiyya's leading figure Refā'i Tāha. He always made sure to communicate with me even at times when he was opposing the initiative. He used to discuss everything with me to understand my point of view and why I support the initiative. He never lost contact with me until he completely disappeared while he was in Syria. May God help him.

6

Islamists Pay for
Zawahiri's Mistakes

Ayman al-Zawahiri's relationship with Osāma bin Lāden has grown deeper, and at the same time his relationship with others in Egypt who witnessed his original two visits to Afghanistan has cooled. I am among the latter.

I supported him in prison in the Jihad case, and this caused me some problems with those who disagreed with his ideas, or did not like his actions. When it was announced that he would be the *ameer* of Egyptian Islamic Jihad in Afghanistan, my support for him again caused me many problems with those who opposed his ideas or disliked him. For example, I was under ruthless attack from Mohamed Ibrahim Mekkawi, a former colonel in the Egyptian Army. Mekkawi was accused in 1987 by the Egyptian authorities of "reviving Islamic jihad." He escaped by fleeing to Afghanistan where he joined Islamic Jihad. Eventually, he left the group due to differences with Zawahiri. Apparently, the two had exchanged accusations regarding who was responsible for the failure of the assassination attempt on former minister of the interior Hassan al-Alfi. Another point of disagreement was that both claimed the loyalties of the Vanguards of Conquest members who were tried by the Higher Military Court in 1994. The two were in the habit of exchanging accusations in the media. The London-based *Al-Hayat* newspaper published an interview with Mekkawi in 1994, in which he accused Zawahiri of being an agent of the CIA, and of cooperating with the Iranians. He also accused him of implementing instructions sent to him by the Egyptian security authorities.

My own problems with Mekkawi began when in an interview with the *Al-Hayat* correspondent in Cairo, Mohamed Salāh, I explained that those accused in the four Vanguards of Conquest cases were in fact loyal to Zawahiri, and that they had nothing to do with Mekkawi. I made this statement because it was true, and not to make a champion out of Zawahiri. Salāh was well aware of the sensitivity of the disagreement between Zawahiri and Mekkawi regarding the Vanguards of Conquest members. For this reason, he agreed to publish the interview he had with me only after having attended a session of one of the four cases and seeing for himself that what I had reported was true: that the accused were loyal to Zawahiri. Salāh himself heard the accused shouting Zawahiri's name and expressing their loyalty to him.

In response, Mekkawi made public accusations against me, despite my friendship with him, and the fact that I was his personal lawyer in Egypt. He accused me, along with Mohamed Salāh, of being agents of Zawahiri. This accusation was serious, as it implied that we were also agents of all those for whom Zawahiri was accused of working. This attack was not prompted by any disagreement on religious or intellectual issues. I never argued with Mekkawi about his activities abroad, the Afghan jihad, nor his history before he left Egypt. His public accusations were the price I paid for telling the truth about Zawahiri and the Vanguards of Conquest members. Zawahiri sent me a message through others that he was happy about my efforts in belying Mekkawi's claims. I made it clear to him at that time that I was not trying to defame Mekkawi and that my only concern was to tell the truth about the Vanguards of Conquest members. In this as in other incidents, my relationship with Zawahiri, while he was in Egypt and after he left, was based on respect and understanding, regardless of our differences in orientation and approach.

Our understanding of each other was reversed when Zawahiri left Afghanistan in 1994 to live with bin Lāden in Sudan. This led to a strengthening of his relationship with bin Lāden, but a cooling of his relationships with the people who knew him in Egypt and who did not follow him to Afghanistan. His close friendship with bin Lāden was met with much criticism from a number of his confidants. When he returned to Afghanistan in 1996, he had become completely different from the man we once knew.

In Sudan, Zawahiri had become part of the environment around him. He was insistent on following the lead of bin Lāden, not only because of the failure of the operations that he had launched in Egypt, but also because of the depleted financial resources of the group. Under Zawahiri's leadship, the group changed from being an organization with the aim of establishing an Islamic state in Egypt, to being a flank of Al-Qaeda; his limelight role changed to that of an assistant. Thus he tied Islamic Jihad, with its long history, to this newer group, which would later deal a severe blow to all Islamic movements and their leaders. The actions of the group had severe ramifications for Islamic organizations and figures whose future plans did not have anything to do with the orientations of Zawahiri and bin Lāden.

I was moved by the confessions of the Islamic Jihad members who were extradited to Egypt in 1988 from Albania, Bulgaria and Azerbaijan. Most of them did not go to these countries to perform any operations or tasks for the group. They went there to find a safe refuge and get a job. Most of them participated only by setting aside a part of their salaries for the group.

Impact of the Gamā'a al-Islāmiyya initiative

One of the results of the Gamā'a al-Islāmiyya initiative, which Zawahiri opposed, was that even before the agreement officially went into effect, the Egyptian authorities stopped their campaign against group members all over Egypt, including those in Upper Egypt. Before the initiative, no Islamist in Egypt had felt safe, and the detention campaigns seemed never ending. At that time, the Egyptian authorities held hundreds or even thousands of members under the pretext that the atmosphere was not suitable for their release. Maltreatment was a common means of taking revenge for the activities of members on the outside. The initiative led to the release of these people after years behind bars, and to considerable improvements in prison conditions for those who were not released. Also, the number of campaigns by the authorities against members of the Gamā'a al-Islāmiyya fell off significantly. The image of the Gamā'a al-Islāmiyya improved in the media and political circles, so much so that a number of public and political figures inimical to Islamic groups called for allowing the Gamā'a al-Islāmiyya to have its own legal entity. This was not even thinkable before the initiative. In Europe, the ceasefire gave the group the status of a repressed political minority, and a number of its leading figures were granted political asylum. Admittedly, all of these developments were not sufficient to appease the struggle. The sacrifices that the group made to achieve this historic change of course deserve more than such small improvements on the part of the authorities. However, I believe that these steps were eventually to be followed by others. Any hope of real progress ended with the incidents of September 11, and the globalization of security that the United States has imposed on the whole world ever since.

Impact of the attacks of September 11, 2001

Islamists across the globe were adversely affected by the September 11 attacks on the United States. Even Islamic movements that did not target the United States are paying the price of this folly. Before my words are misunderstood, I should note that no Islamist or nationalist can be a friend of the United States in view of all the crimes it has committed and continues to commit against Muslims, especially Arab Muslims. A complete overview of these crimes would fill many books. Thus, we all agree that standing up to the United States is an Islamic duty. The point of disagreement among Islamists, and especially between Zawahiri and me, is how best to deal with the world's superpower. Bin Lāden's desire to take revenge heedless of the American and international response, and its effect on the future of the Islamic movements in the world, has given the Americans and other governments the power to destroy the Islamists before our eyes.

Before the September 11 attacks on Washington and New York, bin Lāden and Zawahiri sent their messages to the Americans without giving them legal evidence proving their involvement, starting from the operations performed by bin Lāden's followers in Somalia in 1993, where they fought American soldiers alongside Farrah Idid's forces.

They followed the same policy when they blew up American military locations in Riyadh and Al-Khubar,[1] as well as the American embassies in Nairobi and Darussalam and finally the blowing up of the American destroyer *Cole* in Yemen. In these operations, bin Lāden did not declare his responsibility. All he did was appear on screen a few weeks after each operation to praise each act and its "martyrs" who sacrificed their lives for Islam. He changed this policy of anonymity after September 11, when he appeared on satellite channels threatening the Americans, and tacitly claiming responsibility. Bin Lāden also gave Zawahiri a chance to act as one of the group's leaders by appearing on satellite channels with him and with Abu Ghayth, who talked about a storm of planes. This gave ammunition to the Western media, who started rumors of chemical weapons in the possession of bin Lāden and the Al-Qaeda "army." The Western media also talked about Al-Qaeda's ability to repel any American attack because of the shelter of the treacherous mountain caves that only the Afghans and Arab Afghans knew how to reach.

Many of those who sympathized with the Afghan people demonstrated against the American war. They were shocked to see the Taliban give their weapons to the Northern Alliance forces and then to the Pashtun tribes. The Taliban lost one city after another during the war, until they lost their rule over Afghanistan altogether. Thus, bin Lāden and Zawahiri lost the Taliban, a government that had protected Islamists for many years.

The front pages of international newspapers began to read like obituaries, listing the names of one Islamist after another who was killed by American air strikes or the shelling of the Northern Alliance. The poorly conceived decision to launch the attacks of September 11 created many victims of a war of which they did not choose to be a part. There is no such thing as the Al-Qaeda army. Not all Islamists in Afghanistan are connected to Al-Qaeda, and many of those who were killed never belonged to Al-Qaeda or bin Lāden, and some even disagreed with the man and the ideas of his group. Similarly, the Islamists that traveled to Afghanistan and participated in jihad against the Soviet occupation became victims of bin Lāden and Zawahiri. Thousands of the best young people in the Muslim *umma* chose to

Islamists Pay for Zawahiri's Mistakes

perform their duty of jihad in Afghanistan. They settled there and got married. Because of Zawahiri and bin Lāden, their children were faced with American bombs, although they did not commit any crime.

Before the attacks, the Arabs who had fled to Afghanistan were seen as victims of persecution by the regimes in their countries of origin. This image was transformed by the attacks.

The nagging question that many are now struggling to answer is: Could Zawahiri have expected the strong American response to the attacks on New York and Washington, DC before he planned them – if in fact Al-Qaeda was behind the attacks? I emphasize Zawahiri because I am convinced that he and not bin Lāden is the main player in these events. The answer is that he must not have expected this strong response. The most basic rule of battle is gauging the response of the enemy before taking any action. His miscalculation led him to believe that the American response would be similar to the one engendered by the bombing of the two American embassies in Nairobi and Darussalam, which was restricted to bombing a few places in Afghanistan with missiles. He should have realized that the response would be as grave as was the action. He should have known that in response to the shock that the September 11 attacks caused, the injured lion would try his best to restore his honor, regardless of his image before others.

When I was watching bin Lāden, with Zawahiri behind him, talking about the September 11 attacks, neither directly claiming responsibility nor denying it, I longed for the earlier days of the movement, when Islamic Jihad hurried to claim responsibility for any attack a few hours after it was launched. Many thought that this facilitated the job of the Egyptian security forces by narrowing their investigations of such activities to Islamic Jihad members. But at that time the group did not compromise its principles. Groups announced the truth to everyone because they knew that nothing would befall them except for what God has decreed. Thus, claiming responsibility for military operations was as important to the principals of the group as was the implementation of those operations.

After September 11, bin Lāden and Zawahiri prioritized political and utilitarian considerations over the group principle of claiming responsibility. At the same time, they could not deny responsibility, because denying that they targeted American interests would have embarrassed the Taliban, who gave them refuge. They allowed fear of the American response to deter them from claiming responsibility. The curious fact is that even after the beginning of the American war against Afghanistan, and even after the Taliban was defeated, they continued to neither deny their responsibility in a clear-cut way nor claim it.

Bin Lāden and Zawahiri's behavior was met with a lot of criticism from many Islamists in Egypt and abroad. Some of them contacted me and were very critical of the consequences of the attacks and the lack of clarity as to whether they were behind them or not. A lot of Islamists, including the hawks as well as those supporting the use of peaceful means, opposed Zawahiri's attempts to link Egyptian Islamists to bin Lāden. The hawkish Islamists thought that the American war on Afghanistan shattered any hope that Islamists living outside of Egypt would return to resume their struggle against the Egyptian government. In the post-September 11 world, no countries can afford to be accused of harboring the enemies of the United States. No one ever imagined that a Western European country would extradite Islamists who live on its lands. Before that, Islamists had always thought that arriving in a European city and applying for political asylum was enough to acquire permanent resident status. After September 11, 2001, everything changed. Sweden, for example, extradited Ahmed Hussein 'Ogayza and Mohamed Ibrahim Sulayman al-Zarry. I am worried that more Islamists will be extradited. In Britain, there are many campaigns against the brothers there, akin to the ones that took place in Assyūt, Suhaj and Minya.[2]

It is no secret that I participated with a small effort in helping some brothers get political asylum in Europe, which infuriated the Egyptian government. I struggled to get certificates proving that they were being persecuted in Egypt and I had to fight with officials at some of the European embassies in Cairo because they prolonged the process in order not to enrage the Egyptian government. I also worked with local and international human rights organizations to reduce the pressures on my brothers abroad. When Zawahiri asked me to immigrate to England after he said he would do his best to help me gain political asylum, I refused, knowing that my brothers would lose the work I do for them in Egypt.

Even the Muslim Brotherhood was affected by the American campaign, which targeted everything Islamic. The Americans took measures against the Taqwa Bank,[3] although it has no connections with Al-Qaeda or Islamic Jihad. When Zawahiri criticized the Muslim Brotherhood in his book *The Bitter Harvest*, the group found itself paying the price for an action in which it was not involved. That is why it tried to distance itself from radical Islamists. Instead of trying to achieve 'Abbūd al-Zomor's dream of uniting all Islamic groups, the rift between them increased, making them easy prey for their enemies.

As I am writing this, I do not know whether Zawahiri is alive or not. I know he suffered great hardship during the American war on Afghanistan. I was moved when I received news of the martyrdom of his wife 'Azza Nuwayr and his son Mohamed, who were killed by American bombs. I hope that he survived the American attacks. Nevertheless, we should not ignore the facts, especially after Zawahiri made public parts of conversations that were meant to be private. He left out some facts in order to distort the image of a number of people. Clarifying this distortion is therefore important because it can also help us learn from our mistakes.

The killing of the prominent Gamā'a al-Islāmiyya figures Fareed Sālem Kadwāni and 'Alā' 'Abdel Rāziq by the authorities, despite the peaceful approach the group decided to take, put the group in a difficult position. Everyone waited for the group's response, wondering whether or not members would seek revenge. I condemned the killing of the group's members and so did the group. The peaceful approach was the choice of the Gamā'a al-Islāmiyya and no one pushed members towards their choice, so whatever happened would not have changed their orientation. They believed in the peaceful solution and it was not just a tactic they resorted to to buy time while the group regained its strength. The Gamā'a al-Islāmiyya was wise enough to control its reaction and draw its policies according to its interests without compromising religious and moral principles. It would have been easy for the group to challenge the authorities, an action that would have pleased Zawahiri regardless of the consequences, seeing as he clearly pays little attention to consequences.

I have mentioned earlier Zawahiri's position regarding the leadership of the coalition of the Gamā'a al-Islāmiyya and Islamic Jihad. I also mentioned that Zawahiri was one of the people who brought about the break up of the coalition. Yet Zawahiri, having signed a coalition with Osāma bin Lāden, used the issue of Sheikh 'Omar 'Abdel Rahmān, the leader of the Gamā'a al-Islāmiyya, who is now captive in an American prison, to turn people against the Americans.

I was surprised to see the statements issued by the International Islamic Front for Jihad on the Jews and Crusaders claiming that the issue of Sheikh 'Abdel Rahmān was one of the reasons that led the Front to blow up the American embassies in Nairobi and Darussalam. A couple of years later, bin Lāden and Zawahiri talked in a press conference in Afghanistan about Sheikh 'Abdel Rahmān and convinced his son Mohamed to deliver a speech about his father. Ever since, the security authorities across the world have considered the sheikh's sons Mohamed, known as Assado Allah [the lion of God], and Ahmed, known as Sayfo Allah [the sword of God], to be members of Al-Qaeda, although they were never wanted by any country, including Egypt. The Egyptian authorities never mentioned any role for the sheikh's sons in any of the many court cases against the Gamā'a al-Islāmiyya. This led to the killing of Assado Allah during the American air strikes in Tora Bora, Afghanistan, just a few days after his brother Sayfo Allah was captured by the American authorities. The Americans hyped up his arrest as if they had captured a prominent Al-Qaeda figure to convince the American public that the campaign against Afghanistan was fruitful. We all know that the two sons, who had been in Afghanistan for more than ten years, had never worked for Al-Qaeda or Islamic Jihad. But like hundreds or thousands of Islamists, they paid the price for a mistake that they did not commit. The sheikh's family was already trying to arrange his release from American prisons; they now have to try to release Sayfo Allah as well.

Although the issue of the sheikh is of paramount importance to everyone, it is still an affair of the Gamā'a al-Islāmiyya, which chose him to be its leader. The group had been doing its best to get him released, not to increase pressure on him. The group implemented many operations in Egypt until the Luxor operation in 1997 and it could have directed one of its operations towards an American target whether inside or outside Egypt. But the group, with judicious vision based on accurate calculations, realized that any action against American interests would not help the sheikh. They knew that he would be harmed by any action against American interests.

When the imprisoned historic leaders of the Gamā'a al-Islāmiyya read the statement issued in *Al-Hayat* in February 1998 about the establishment of the International Islamic Front for Jihad on the Jews and Crusaders, and noticed that Refā'i Tāha had signed the charter of the organization, they sent a message to him through me. The message contained a lot of criticism of the Front and the ideas and objectives that were mentioned in its charter. They also asked him to inform them of his reasons for signing the charter and including the name of the Gamā'a al-Islāmiyya in a coalition that seeks to achieve objectives that were never on the group's agenda. This explains why Tāha at the end of July 1998 issued a statement saying that he never signed the charter. Tāha said that he was asked on the phone whether he would sign a statement to support the Iraqi people who were under American air strikes and he agreed. Unfortunately, Zawahiri refused to comment on this in his statements or his last book. He avoided any reference to anything that might embarrass them.

Since joining the Islamist movement, my main objective has been the elevation of Islam and helping my fellow Islamists from all Islamic groups. For that reason, the Egyptian authorities and the international press have found it difficult to categorize me. When I help an Islamic Jihad member, they put me under Islamic Jihad, only to see me defending Gamā'a al-Islāmiyya members as well as helping people who do not belong to any group to gain political asylum in a European country.

7

Executing a Boy and Killing a Prominent Group Leader

All the threads that lead to Islamic Jihad leaders stop at a certain point and are lost. Those lost threads lead to Dr. 'Abdel Mu'iz, the code name that the members used to refer to Ayman al-Zawahiri.

Islamic Jihad is made up of several committees, each of which is headed by one of Zawahiri's close confidants. For instance, the Financial Committee is charged with finding resources to support the activities of the group, as well as deciding how the money should be allocated. There is also the Civil Committee, which deals with recruitment of new members. This requires researching them, categorizing them and determining the best ways to contact them. The Military Committee deals specifically with recruiting cadres from the Egyptian Army, and the *Shari'a* Committee is charged with issuing *fatwa*, in addition to doing research. The work of the *Shari'a* Committee is positively related to the increase of armed activity because it is the committee that has to announce the religious justification for any armed operations of the group. It also deals with responding to the criticism of the media and opposing political powers.

The tight security policy of Islamic Jihad is understandable in light of its clear agenda to clash with the regime. Any arrest of members is an opportunity for information to be extracted through torture. Such information could include anything from the activities of the group and its plans to the leadership hierarchy. This is why each member knows only his own role. When the members pledge their obedience and loyalty to the leader of the group, they are aware that they are not supposed to ask any questions about things that are not directly related to their role. There are always a few curious members who ask too many questions. The leaders of the group keep an eye on them to make sure that they do not get this information. A number of highly skilled and efficient recruits were not allowed to join because their curiosity was viewed as a threat to the security of the group.

The tight security arrangements of Islamic Jihad have successfully allowed it to increase its activities despite the number of threats to its security arrangement over the past few years. These include the arrest of dozens of members in the Vanguards of Conquest case, the arrest and extradition of the Albania-based members and the extradition from Azerbaijan of Ahmed Salāma Mabrūk. The group has thus far always found good replacements for the leading members that were arrested. The group has also succeeded in changing its plans and style whenever information has been extracted from its members. However, Zawahiri has made some mistakes mainly due to the abnormal conditions under which he has been living since he left Egypt. He has had to move from one place to another, which involves infiltrating through borders and being chased. Zawahiri has always insistently preferred his own opinion despite his humbleness. He has always tended to get into clashes with those who do not agree with him, despite his tolerance. This has led to some rifts in the group.

In his book *Knights Under the Banner of the Prophet*, Zawahiri opened many files that had long been closed, and rubbed salt into many wounds. He discussed many thorny issues, but ignored many others. The result was that his book did not show the whole picture, thereby blurring and distorting the truth. The Islamic movement has been subject to so many dangers that Islamists have had reason to be constantly concerned about its future. For this reason, we have learned to separate our personal differences from the group's interests. Zawahiri has revealed information that might harm and embarrass others, tarnishing the image of some Islamists. He has opened these files, forcing me to comment on them. I will address three incidents that have been vague. Two are related to the Security Committee and the third is related to Zawahiri himself.

Executing a boy

Islamists such as myself have always lamented to God the life sentences that civil and military courts issue against our fellow Islamists. We have urged human rights organizations to pressure the Egyptian government to stop the shedding of Islamists' blood. We have brought forth many suits asking for justice for Islamists. In his articles, books and press statements, Zawahiri has always criticized civil and military courts that sentenced the members of his group to death. However, Zawahiri became so cruel that he killed the son of one of his closest confidants in front of his father. The boy was condemned by a *shari'a* court that Zawahiri formed. The court said that he harmed the group by spying on its activities for the Egyptian authorities. I remember when I heard the news about the execution of the boy, I did not believe the person who told me the story and accused him of lying because he had a grudge against Zawahiri, and of trying to tarnish his image. Unfortunately, I discovered that it was true. The boy, 15-year-old Mos'ab Mohamed Sharaf, was executed in front of a number of leading figures within the group in order to deter others from committing the same crime, which Zawahiri considered unforgivable.

The Security Committee in Islamic Jihad had jurisdiction in the boy's case because it deals with the security of the group. When Zawahiri was living in Sudan with Osāma bin Lāden along with hundreds of Islamic Jihad members, the committee noticed that information was being leaked to the Egyptian authorities. This information included the activities of the group and the places that Zawahiri and his men frequented. Some members of the committee noticed that the house where Zawahiri was living in Khartoum was being watched by the Egyptian authorities. Islamic Jihad preempted an attempt on the life of Zawahiri when a bomb was planted at the entrance of a hospital that he frequented. After conducting some investigations, the committee discovered that the Egyptian authorities had managed to infiltrate the group to the extent that they knew what happened in the meetings of the leading figures in the group. The Egyptian authorities had recruited the young Sharaf, son of one of the leading figures in the group by the name of Mohamed Sharaf, by taking photos of him in a compromising position and had blackmailed him into spying on the group. This took place in 1994, when Zawahiri was living in Sudan. Sudanese intelligence played an active role in this story, as they were the ones who discovered that he was spying for the Egyptian authorities. The Sudanese government knew that Egyptian intelligence was active in Sudan, but avoided revealing such information in public. A Sudanese official informed Zawahiri of the matter, and he in turn referred the case to the Security Committee.

Some of Zawahiri's close aides said that he was very moved by this incident and that he spent a lot of time talking to Mohamed Sharaf, the boy's father, trying to alleviate his pain. Others attributed Sharaf's decision to leave the group to this incident. Sharaf was in a very difficult position. As a top-ranking figure in the group, he had to attend the execution of his son by gunfire. Zawahiri also asked him to deal with the consequences of the shooting with the Sudanese authorities, especially after some Sudanese officials were angry at the establishment of a *shari'a* court and using Zawahiri's law on Sudanese soil. The Sudanese government was also concerned that the Egyptian authorities would take revenge for the death of their young agent.

This incident shows how the cruel life that Zawahiri has lived has affected his character. In Zawahiri's mind, Islamic Jihad has turned from being a means to achieving an end into being an end in and of itself. The execution of the boy prioritized the deterrence of members from any temptation to betray the security of the group over all else, including humanitarian considerations and even over the possibility of Sharaf leaving the group.

The execution of Abu Khadeega

I have mentioned earlier that when Zawahiri was arrested after the assassination of Sadāt, he was forced to reveal the martyr 'Esām al-Qamari's whereabouts under torture, which helped the Egyptian authorities to arrest him. This incident was a great burden on Zawahiri, who had had a very close relationship with Qamari. We, like Qamari himself, never thought of blaming Zawahiri because we know that he only told the authorities about his whereabouts under terrible torture. Whenever we talked about the assassination of Sadāt, we avoided talking about the circumstances that led to the arrest of Qamari in order not to cause Zawahiri more pain.

When the tables were turned, Zawahiri's treatment of one of the prominent figures of Islamic Jihad was quite different from that which he had experienced. Suffering from the pain of torture, Mohamed 'Abdel 'Aleem, known amongst Egyptian Islamists as Abu Khadeega, informed the Egyptian authorities of the whereabouts of another member, enabling them to arrest him. Abu Khadeega was one of the most loyal members of Islamic Jihad. Throughout the 1980s, he was held in high esteem because of his good manners and for favoring his fellow Islamists over himself. Before joining Islamic Jihad and working with Zawahiri in Afghanistan, he was a good friend of Abu 'Obayda al-Bensheeri ('Ali al-Rasheedi). Rasheedi wanted to serve the Islamist movement without working within an organization. As soon as he arrived in Afghanistan, he joined Osāma bin Lāden's Al-Qaeda and moved up through the organization until he became its military leader. He was martyred by drowning in Lake Victoria. Abu Khadeega and Rasheedi were so close that the latter made the travel arrangements for the former to go to Afghanistan. In Afghanistan, Abu Khadeega joined Islamic Jihad and worked directly with Zawahiri himself. He worked in an orphanage in Peshawar in Pakistan. Although he was only 25 at the time, he was very active and played an important role in the group.

Heading for Afghanistan, he had to leave behind a wife and children. He missed them terribly and he was worried about them throughout his stay in Afghanistan. He expressed to Zawahiri his wish to go back to Egypt to see them and try to bring them to Afghanistan. Zawahiri tried to talk Abu Khadeega out of traveling for fear that he would be arrested by the Egyptian authorities, but his resolve was firm. The Security Committee made a plan to return him to Egypt on a forged passport with an itinerary that passed through a number of countries before arriving in Egypt, in order to make it difficult for the Egyptian authorities to track him. Despite these measures, as soon as he arrived at the airport, he was arrested by the Egyptian authorities, who tortured him terribly until they extracted information about the activities of the group. Abu Khadeega told the authorities about the hiding place of the prominent Islamic Jihad figure 'Esām 'Abdel Gayyid, who had infiltrated into Egypt to achieve certain aims. Soon thereafter, 'Abdel Gayyid was arrested. He is still in prison today.

Although there was no evidence that Abu Khadeega's confession was the reason behind 'Abdel Gayyid's arrest, the response to the confession among Islamic Jihad members was exceptionally cruel. At the time, Islamic Jihad was going through a period in which it was trying to utilize Afghanistan to complete its organizational structure. Zawahiri and the members of the Security Committee were trying more earnestly than ever to deter members from harming the group.

The Egyptian authorities eventually released Abu Khadeega, and after lengthy judicial procedure, he received his passport. After his release, he lived in Boolaq al-Dakroor where I was living at the time. I met with him many times. He told me that other members had been treating him terribly since his release, at the instigation of Zawahiri, he thought. I advised him to bring his wife and children from Saudi Arabia to live in Egypt for a while, at least until he found a way to confirm that Zawahiri did not bear grudges against him. Abu Khadeega was a very stubborn man, and despite my advice he insisted on joining his family in Saudi Arabia, where he bumped into Zawahiri in the Holy Mosque. He explained to Zawahiri that what was revealed was done under the pain of torture, and that he did not mean to cause the arrest of 'Abdel Gayyid. Zawahiri treated him coldly. Still, Abu Khadeega returned to Afghanistan to work for the same orphanage. A few weeks later, he traveled to Islamabad en route to Jeddah to bring his family to Afghanistan. He was hosted by Pakistan's Islamist group Harakat ul-Ansār. He then disappeared in Pakistan. Islamic Jihad spread rumors that he died in a car accident. They claimed that he had a car that he used for his travels between Islamabad and Peshawar. Many people, however, said that there was no accident and that the members of the Security Committee in Islamic Jihad pretended they wanted to have him meet someone away from where he was hosted by Harakat ul-Ansār. He disappeared soon after this. Some fellow Islamists expressed their sorrow at the way the group liquidated Abu Khadeega. A leading Islamist figure called me from abroad and asked me whether I helped

Abu Khadeega leave Egypt. I felt that the inquirer wanted to know if I was involved in his liquidation. This incident is still a subject of controversy until now.

The resignation game

Zawahiri threatened to resign from the leadership of Islamic Jihad in February 1998, in a move to silence those leading figures in the group who disagreed with his decision to join the International Islamic Front for Jihad on the Jews and Crusaders with Osāma bin Lāden. In the history of Islamic movements we have never seen a leader exert such pressure on his followers to accept what he has decreed, regardless of their opinion. A number of fellow Islamists told me that Zawahiri followed the lead of Osāma bin Lāden, oblivious to the objections of other members who believed that precipitating a confrontation with the United States would harm the group and destroy the bases it had established in several countries. They also thought that this confrontation would reduce the activities of the group in Egypt. They argued that the group should not involve itself in bin Lāden's efforts to settle scores with the United States, and that performing the duty of helping him against the Americans would endanger the future of Islamic Jihad as well as the lives of its members.

Some members told me that Zawahiri's justifications were not convincing to them. He argued that the Front would facilitate the achievement of the main objective of the group: the institution of Islamic *shari'a*. He argued that members were too unwilling to enter into confrontations in which they saw any potential losses. He wanted to show the peoples of Muslim countries that while their governments cower before the dictates of the United States, Islamists do not fear it. He believed that once Muslims saw proof of their boldness, the Islamic *umma* would support the Front. Due to this difference, a number of members froze their activity.

Zawahiri forced acquiescence by threatening to resign. This was a game he played, knowing the result. In the earlier days of the organization, the financial resources of the group had always come from members. The successive failures of the group in Egypt and the arrest of most of its members had dried up these sources, leaving the group reliant mainly on bin Lāden's money, which was assured through Zawahiri's connection to him. The members knew that if this stream stopped flowing, the group would lose its last source of support, and would cease to exist. The group found itself with only one option: to refuse his resignation.

8

The Struggle Continues

Most Islamists around the globe, especially in Egypt, agree that Zawahiri's policies have caused a crisis, with which Islamic groups all over the world must now contend. The September 11 attacks on New York and Washington mark a new era with new challenges to Islamists, who need to understand these challenges. The Americans have made clear their intention to wipe out all Islamist groups, even if they are not connected with Al-Qaeda, Osāma bin Lāden and Zawahiri. The attacks have met with doubts as to their religious justification and political significance. They have also raised questions regarding the future of Islamist groups and their ability to face up to the new challenges that resulted from the attacks, including the War on Afghanistan and the determination of the West to track down members of Islamist groups across the globe. The attacks gave rise to a new kind of globalization: the globalization of security. Western countries are working to improve their relations with Arab and Islamic countries in order to cooperate in rounding up Islamists. The attacks have allowed the West to tarnish the image of Islam by equating it with violence and Al-Qaeda.

There is no doubt that the United States was alarmed by the dialogue aired by Osāma bin Lāden and Zawahiri in the Arab and Muslim media, and by its popularity in the Muslim world. The most popular of their statements were those regarding the Palestinian cause, which is thwarted both by the stubborn Zionist arrogance and the unflinching resolve on the part of the Americans to continue their policies. The issue is one of the closest to the hearts of the people in Arab and Muslim societies. Zawahiri's message to the American people, in which he talked about the injustice done to the Arabs and Muslims due to

American policies, won him much public support. He gave examples such as the air strikes against the Iraqi people and the genocide committed against the Iraqi children. He also mentioned the conspiracy against the territorial unity of Sudan, supported by the crusader John Garang, as well as the American efforts to control Sudan. It is true that the words of Zawahiri and bin Lāden were aimed at awakening the dormant *umma*, and reviving the Islamic civilization that predates other civilizations. These issues are indeed important to every Arab and every Muslim, and deserve concerted efforts on our part. The Arab layman is unhappy with the poor state of the Muslim *umma*, which exceeds a billion people. The Palestinian cause should always be at the top of the priorities of the Islamist movement. We should look for ways to unify the Arab and Muslim countries in the struggle to mobilize the many capabilities necessary to liberate the occupied lands; then the unity of the Arabs will turn the Palestinians into a power that can take back its rights.

The type of dialogue that Al-Qaeda used with the media must be avoided. So too should we abandon the approach of bin Lāden and Zawahiri in which the main objective is to administer as much harm to the United States as possible. This has involved, thus far, launching attacks on American targets in Nairobi and Darussalam in 1998, the bombing of the destroyer *Cole* off the Yemeni shores, and the September 11 attacks on New York and Washington. Such attacks are not an effective approach to solving the deep problems that mark the struggle between the Muslim civilization and the racist, crusader, Western civilization. Our approach should focus on the achievement of Islamic unity, not on launching temporary attacks that divide us, with some supporting and some against. We should make balanced policies, and establish a front that stretches along the man-made borders of the Muslim world. We must work to avoid alienating any organization or individual that has a real desire to win the battle against the enemies of Islam.

The Islamist movement has gone through a number of hardships during different historical periods. It has clashed with several governments and rulers in different political epochs. Its leaders have always been pursued and persecuted by the powers that be. The Islamist

The Road to Al-Qaeda

movement has occasionally suffered from a fossilization of its followers, in which they accept the prevailing ideology without question. The movement suffers when there is a lack of *ijtihād* [independent judgment] as a source of knowledge. Despite these hardships, the Islamist movement has always won its battles with the forces of tyranny and suppression. Such battles have always been followed by a renewed vigor.

The following brief summary of the history of the Islamic movement will reveal that all the attempts to eradicate Islamist groups have failed, regardless of the ruthlessness of security arrangements.

Even during the weak periods of the Islamic state and the caliphate under the Ottomans, Islamic figures played an important role in leading the public to fight occupation, preserve their Islamic heritage, and even spread the teachings of Islam. The Ottoman sultan 'Abdel Hameed struggled to consolidate the Islamic nation, through the establishment of a league of Islamic states. Such figures resisted Napoleon Bonaparte's occupation of Egypt in 1798, and his attempts to replace the Islamic Egyptian identity with French principles mixed with a set of Islamic Egyptian principles.

Bonaparte claimed that the goal of the French campaign was to defend the Egyptians against the Mameluks. Some of the leaders of his campaign even claimed that they converted to Islam in order to convince the Egyptians that their intentions were good. These gestures of the French did not mislead the scholars of Al-Azhar at the time, nor did they mislead the governor of Alexandria, Mohamed Kurayyim, who opposed the campaign and was hanged for it. He was followed by others who led the public to fight jihad against colonialism by struggling against the French campaign, including 'Omar Makram, Sheikh al-Sadāt, Quwisni and Abdullah al-Sharqāwi. Strangely, officials from the Ministry of Culture, with the support of some writers and historians, wanted to celebrate the golden anniversary of the French campaign against Egypt. They claimed that the campaign carried the banners of enlightenment and culture to the country.

Gamāleddine al-Afghani [1838–1897] brought about an Islamic awakening at a time when there were many attempts to destroy the Islamic caliphate. Some people cast doubts on his beliefs. He had a lot of skills, including wide knowledge of religious subjects such as Islamic jurisprudence, Koranic interpretation and *hadeeth* [the traditions of the Prophet including his habits and sayings attributed to him]. He was also well versed in the sciences of politics, sociology and philosophy. Some people are critical of Afghani because he was interested in Western civilization, but in my opinion it never affected his deep commitment to his Islamic heritage.

Mohamed Rasheed Reda [1865–1935], publisher of the magazine *Al-Manar*, also played an important role in supporting the old Islamic principles, and opposing attempts to Westernize the legal system in Egypt instead of using Islamic *shari'a*. He opposed the calls to do away with the Islamic caliphate. His book *Al-Khilafa aw Al-Imāma al-'Oliya* [*The Caliphate or the High Imamate*] is an important reference for researchers in the field of modernizing the Islamic state. He made many contributions updating Islamic concepts for the modern world.

Most of the attempts at Islamic revival started in Egypt. Hassan al-Banna [founder of the Muslim Brotherhood, who lived 1906–1949] called for Islamic revival at the beginning of the twentieth century, following the collapse of the caliphate and Kemal Ataturk's success in destroying any trace of it. He presented a modern vision of a form of Islamic unity. Banna was influenced greatly by the writings of Mohamed Rasheed Reda in *Al-Manar*. Banna became a torch of light at a time where the darkness of secular thinking prevailed and preoccupied the Egyptian intellect. He managed to propagate his beliefs about Islamic unity, which permeated to the roots of Egyptian society in a short space of time. He moved from Isma'eeliyya, where he worked as an elementary school teacher, to Cairo, where he established the Muslim Brotherhood.

Sayyid Qutb was a significant contributor to the *jihādi* Islamist philosophy, which counterbalanced the attempts of secularization and Westernization, in the form of Gamāl 'Abdel Nasser's tyranny. Nasser instituted a program of "upgrading" Al-Azhar, by changing the process of selecting the Grand Sheikh of Al-Azhar from an electoral process within the institution to a system of government appointment. Nasser changed the financial aspects of the position of the Grand Sheikh by replacing the system of compensation from the *awqāf* with the payment of a "salary" from the state. Al-Azhar lost the independence that it once enjoyed, minimizing its political contribution. These changes destroyed the role of Al-Azhar in encouraging people to rise against political oppression and the attempts to obliterate Egypt's Islamic identity.

The June 1967 defeat broke this period of political suppression, giving breathing room to young people searching for their identity. The era of Nasser's tyranny was only a brief disruption in the line of generations of leaders of the Islamic revival, which was resumed when Ayman al-Zawahiri emerged to lead the first clandestine cell in 1966. The main objective of the cell was to institute Islamic *shari'a* by force. The *jihādi* Islamic movement that he spearheaded produced thousands of *mujāhideen* such as Kareem al-Anadoli, who contributed to further developing *jihādi* Islamic thinking.

Anwar al-Sadāt introduced a morsel of freedom by releasing the Muslim Brotherhood members who had been held in prison. This freedom gave new prominence to a number of Islamist leaders who carried the torch of Islamic revival and helped establish the contemporary Islamist groups. Following the years of reconciliation and harmony between Sadāt and the Islamists came years of clashing. Sadāt was assassinated on October 6, 1981 by Khāled al-Islamboli and his fellow Islamists 'Abdel Hameed 'Abdel Salām, Hussein 'Abbās and 'Ata Tāyel Hameeda.

Mohamed 'Abdel Salām Farag was a pioneer in reviving the concept of the "absent duty," meaning jihad. Following Sadāt's assassination, Islamist groups grew all the more powerful. They became more able to connect with the Egyptian people. They were conspicuous in universities, syndicates, sporting clubs and poor areas. The slogan "*Islam huwa al-hall*," meaning "Islam is the answer," characterized this period in which the Islamist trend was very strong.

All of the noise about the "clash of civilizations" started in the West, when Richard Nixon wrote in his book a warning to his readers of the main enemy of the West: Islam. These warnings were echoed in the words of the former secretary general of NATO. It is therefore hard to believe that George Bush's use of the word "crusade" regarding the American war on Afghanistan was merely a slip of the tongue. The word revealed his deeper intentions, and revealed that the war that was

The Struggle Continues　　　　　　　　　　**115**

in the works was indeed a crusade. It is worth noting that the British prime minister Tony Blair echoed the same words.

Because of the resilience of the Islamist cause, society and its intelligentsia in the nationalist movement must connect with Islamic groups, rather than clashing with them. Similarly, we, with our ancient heritage of tolerance towards minorities that live with us but do not share the same Islamic faith, must get used to different opinions. This statement should not be misconstrued. My appreciation for and belief in the Islamist cause is beyond doubt. My devotion to this cause is a religious and ideological choice, as well as a political view. It is a religious and ideological necessity as well as an expression of our identity. The law that Egyptians have chosen is Islam and on this point they will never change their mind. The contentment of the people is more important than man-made laws.

To ensure success for Islamist groups, their leaders should be given space for self-criticism. I would like to repeat what I said when the Gamā'a al-Islāmiyya launched its ceasefire initiative: yes to self-criticism, but no to backing off. This philosophy is in line with the majority of Muslim scholars. It is for the further invigoration of the movement that I argue for the protection of the right of anyone who takes Islam to be his religion and practices it to openly discuss issues facing the faith.

Our brethren, the leaders of Islamist groups living in European countries, should play a pivotal role in studying the current developments. They should probe into the mistakes that led us to our present position. They should form an Islamic bloc to replace the current separate factions, and to protect the identity of the *umma*, which is threatened by a ruthless crusade. No matter how strong the various Islamist groups are as separate entities, they need to unite to achieve success. Only by uniting into one entity can these groups face up to this onslaught. When I proposed the issue of unity to a number of fellow Islamists living in Europe, they agreed, but the majority of them preferred to wait for a while. They were worried that their efforts would be construed as a way of settling scores with Zawahiri or bin Lāden.

*　　*　　*

The Road to Al-Qaeda

During the era of the first Islamic state, the first Muslim leader was at the helm: the Prophet Mohamed. Under him, the Muslims were defeated only once, when the soldiers did not listen to their leader in the Battle of Uhud. The defeat was dangerous to the Islamic entity. Many Muslim leaders were killed and rumors spread that Mohamed himself had been killed too.

In the Battle of Hunayn, thousands of Muslim soldiers were sure of victory because of their large numbers. Athough they thought they could not be defeated, in the end they were, because God wanted to teach them that the material advantage in a war, although it is important, does not bring victory by itself. Whatever they have in terms of weapons and soldiers, God will grant Muslims victory only if their hearts follow His path. As human beings, Muslims are like any others in that if they do not work hard, they do not excel in material power. This reality was expressed clearly by a great Muslim leader from the early post-Islamic era, when the Islamic empire was a formidable power. He told his soldiers shortly before a battle, "You have to be pious to God, because if you have the same sins as your enemies, they will outdo you with the weapons they have."

The most important characteristic of Muslim societies is that when they are defeated, they still have faith that they will eventually be victorious. They know that their defeat does not detract from the soundness of the Muslim faith. God, Glorified be His name, said in the Koran:

> [What is the matter with you?] When a single disaster smites you, although you smote [your enemies] with one twice as great you say: "From where does this come to us?" Say [to them], "It is from yourselves [because of your evil deeds]."[1]

If we see defeat as only a temporary state from which Muslim society will manage to recover quickly, in time to win the next battle, a loss can serve as a healthy development. Each recovery from defeat is proof that Muslim society is capable of outgrowing its weaknesses by addressing and strengthening the areas that allowed for defeat.

Thus, we should not give in to this defeat. We should not turn our backs away from the path of God. The Koran said, "O you who believe! Whoever from among you turns back from his religion [Islam], Allah will bring a people whom He will love and they will love Him; humble towards the believers, stern towards the disbelievers."[2] On the contrary, all our efforts and resources should be pooled to overcome this ordeal. New means and strategies other than those that led to the defeat should be utilized in order to continue our mission. God said in the Koran,

O you who believe! When you meet those who disbelieve, in a battle-field, never turn your backs to them. And whoever turns his back to them on such a day – unless it be a stratagem of war, or to retreat to a troop [of his own], – he indeed has drawn upon himself wrath from Allah. And his abode is Hell, and worst indeed is that destination![3]

The style in which the Muslim battalion operates must change according to circumstances, just as *fatwa* can change according to place, time and circumstances, according to Islamic scholars. When they are weak, Muslims may proceed at the pace of the slowest of the group. They should not neglect Islam as a way of life, nor should they overlook any of its established pillars. Rather, they should strive to behave as the Prophet Mohamed (peace be upon him) did, when he was in a position of weakness in Mecca before he migrated to Medina. The behavior of the Prophet Mohamed while he was in Mecca was completely different from his actions once he arrived in Medina. Similarly, there was a great difference between his actions before and after the conquest of Mecca. Before the conquest of Mecca, he accepted the Hudaybiya Treaty, taking care not to accept anything against the dictates of Islam. A state of weakness requires Muslims to act carefully so as to pass through the period with minimum losses. "And fear the *fitnah* [affliction and trial] which affects not in particular [only] those of you who do wrong [but it may afflict all the good and the bad people], and know that Allah is Severe in punishment."[4]

Defeat can afflict Muslim society just as it does other societies, and all things are predestined by God. When Muslims suffer the sting of defeat, their loss of confidence can snowball into further deterioration. The other option is for Muslims to continue their jihad while working hard to avoid repeating the mistakes that led to the defeat. Defeat has the potential to shatter morals and increase the number of destructive voices. It can also put unqualified cadres in positions of leadership, while those who are qualified become ineffective. Defeat can also close the minds of the people to the opinions of others. In these cases, defeat becomes like a chronic disease that is characterized by the following traits:

Feeling far from God

The first of these traits is that people stray far from the path of God and cease to use His *shari'a* as the system of rules to settle the disputes that erupt between individuals. God Almighty has ordained for us the principles that should be followed in case of any disputes that might afflict the Muslim battalion. The Koran tells us, "O you who believe! Answer Allah [by obeying Him] and [His] Messenger when he [peace be upon him] calls you to that which will give you life."[5] God also said, "But no, by your Lord, they can have no Faith, until they make you [O Muhammad] judge in all disputes between them."[6] The Prophet Mohamed also said, "I have left in you what if you hold tight to, you shall never go astray: the Koran and my traditions."

Excessive pride of each person regarding his own opinion

This comes out of a decreasing emphasis on religion, which corresponds to a decreasing feeling of being watched over by God. "Is then He [Allah] Who takes charge [guards, maintains, provides] of every person and knows all that he has earned?"[7] One of our venerable forefathers once said, "Do not consider God the least important one who is watching you." When the feeling of being watched declines, the normal result is to cease to use God's *shari'a* in daily affairs and in solving jurisprudence and intellectual disputes. The lack of this feeling also leads to an increased emphasis on human opinion as the source of truth, and especially one's own opinion. When God's presence seems distant, people do not try to accommodate differences of opinion. All these factors break the unity of Muslims, which would otherwise be the main way to victory, and the source of the courage that motivates us to rise to the challenge of other competing civilizations.

Mutual hatred and differences

The wisdom that God has taught to all generations of the Muslim *umma*, since the Prophet's *hijra* [migration] to Mecca to establish the Islamic state, is love for God. The first brick in the construction of this strong state is love for God and the brotherhood between the *muhājireen* [the people who migrated with the Prophet] and the *ansār* [the people of Medina who received the *muhājireen*]. The strongest stage of faith is when one both loves and hates for the sake of God. Whoever gives for God and withholds giving for God has reached the highest state of believing. The people who can achieve victory are those that love God and are loved by him. Love is their slogan. It is an invincible sword that can bring about victory. No group in either the Eastern or Western blocs, can seize this weapon. God said in the Koran, "If you had spent all that is in the earth, you could not have united their hearts, but Allah has united them."[8] Those who will be victorious are "humble towards the believers, stern towards the disbelievers," God said. Thus, back-stabbing amongst the soldiers of the contemporary Islamic revival is the main reason for its inability to achieve its aims.

Differences between the many groups

One of our sheikhs says it is healthy that there are many groups. To him, it is a sign of the vitality of the Islamic revival. He likened Islam to a high building that has many floors and windows, but has one door. The many floors and windows are Islamist groups and societies. This image would be accurate if the numerous Islamist groups pooled their resources and capabilities to achieve a unified goal, and if each group accepted the possibility that developments would prove the opinions of its members faulty, as did our forefathers in the old glorious days of Islam. The variety of groups would be a positive aspect of the movement if they accommodated differences of opinion, and if they were polite in the face of disagreement. The diversity of groups and perspectives becomes a disadvantage when it results in accusations, disagreement, and a general lack of tolerance for opposing opinions. The bitter reality of Islamist groups is that each group believes that its voice is the only one qualified to speak on behalf of Islam and the Islamist trend. The groups do not cooperate for the well-being of the Muslim world.

The rampancy of misdeeds and sins

I have mentioned earlier what a great Muslim leader from the earlier post Islamic times told his soldiers, "You have to be pious to God, because if you have the same sins as your enemies, they will outdo you with the weapons they have." While the Islamist movement is looking for the reasons for its long-standing defeat, it is required to repent to God for the misdeeds and sins that its members have committed, soldiers and leaders alike. Some misdeeds are committed by an individual, but they affect the whole *umma*. We should not overlook this element, which is an important factor in the defeat. We should not belittle the small misdeeds. An old poet said: "To be a pious person, do not overlook misdeeds, small or big – mountains are only small pebbles."

When the Muslim Sultan Qutuz wanted to make an army to fight the Mongols, he asked the well-known scholar at the time 'Ezz Ibn 'Abdel Salām to declare jihad and tout the war efforts. Sheikh Ibn 'Abdel Salam did not only interact with the emotional side of this request. He asked Qutuz to lead a campaign into the streets and into the whorehouses and shops of the sellers of alcohol to break the pots of alcohol and close down the whorehouses.

The moral behind this story is that any group that hoists the banner of Islam and the oneness of God should have a number of qualities to effect victory. God did not promise victory to anyone who claims wrongly to be a believer. The Koran says, "Say: 'O Ibadi [my slaves] who have transgressed against themselves [by committing evil deeds and sins]! Despair not of the Mercy of Allâh: verily, Allâh forgives all sins. Truly, He is Oft-Forgiving, Most Merciful.'"[9]

Fossilization, imitation and the lack of *ijtihād*

The most important characteristic of Islam compared with other religions is that it is suitable for all times. The Koran contains general principles that the *umma* can interpret through looking at the reasons why the verses were revealed, as well as looking at the *sunna* as an important source of legislation, and a guide in interpretation of the Koran. It is most dangerous for a defeated generation to cease to believe in the importance of the modern sciences, and to stop following recent scientific developments. God permitted people to learn sciences as long as they do not violate divine precepts. The main characteristic of a defeated generation is that it abides by one interpretation of the Koran and *sunna*, which should not hold because of the change of milieu. This gives rise to some *fatwa* that call for isolationism and that forbid the use of sciences that benefit humanity. Some of them go so far as to forbid education and the holding of a government post. This defeated generation has concerned itself excessively with such unimportant issues while ignoring some much more important ones. A poet said, "They talk like 'Antara,[10] but when it comes to actions they are [motionless] like a pole."

In the midst of the frustration of defeat, there is a tendency to take events at face value. Frustration breeds the prevalence of slogans that do not offer any productive alternatives, and leads to overlooking the importance of investigating how the early Muslims dealt with similar situations. If we look at Islamic history, we will find that the Muslim army was shaken badly in the Battle of Mu'ata. The three leaders that the Prophet assigned to lead the army died. Khāled Ibn al-Waleed took leadership of the army, even though he was not assigned to do so. He organized the army lines and made a decision to withdraw. He was not influenced by the criticism that he received for withdrawing. The Prophet supported his decision when he knew about it.

The faithful members of the Islamist movement should try to heal the wounds caused by some of its members, who took charge of the political and media dialogue of the movement. They spoke on behalf of the whole movement, leading it astray. These faithful members should also isolate important causes from unimportant ones in order to achieve our aims. These aims include the need of the Muslim *umma* to keep abreast of modern civilization in a lofty Islamic framework.

Notes

Introduction

1. L. Carl Brown, *Religion and State: The Muslim Approach to Politics* (New York: Columbia University Press, 2000), 27.
2. *Ibid.*, 33.
3. Burhan Ghalyun, "al-Islam wa azmat 'alaqat al-sultah al-ijtima'iyyah," in 'Abd al-Baqi al-Hirmasi et al., *al-Din fi' l mujtama' al-'arabi* (Beirut: Markaz Dirasat al-Wih*dah al-ëArabiyyah, 1990), 305. See also Ghalyun, *Le malaise arabe: l'État contre la nation* (Paris: La Découverte, 1991).
4. Ahmad Kamal Abu'l Majd, "Surat al-hhalah al-islamiyyah 'ala masharif alfiyyah jadidah," *Wijhat Nadhar*, volume 1(11), December, 1999, 6.
5. On this point, see Muhammad Mahdi Shams al-Din, *Fiqh al-'unf al-musallah fi' l Islam* (Beirut: al-Mu'assassah al-Dawliyyah li'l Dirasat wa'l Nashr, 2001).
6. In explaining the September 11, 2001 attacks on the United States, Anderson argues:

> The Republican administration is as well aware as anyone on the Left that September 11 was not simply an act of unmotivated evil, but a response to the widely disliked role of the United States in the Middle East. This is a region in which – unlike Europe, Russia, China, Japan or Latin America – there are virtually no regimes with a credible base to offer effective transmission points for American cultural or economic hegemony. The assorted Arab states are docile enough, but they lack any kind of popular support, resting on family networks and secret police which typically compensate for their factual servility to the US with a good deal of media hostility, not to speak of closure, towards America. Uniquely, indeed, Washington's oldest dependency and most valuable client in the region, Saudi Arabia, is more barricaded against US cultural penetration than any country in the world after North Korea. Perry Anderson, "Force and Consent," *New Left Review*, number 17 (September/October, 2002), 16.

7. See, for example, Aftab A. Malik, ed., *Shattered Illusions: Analyzing the War on Terrorism* (Bristol, England: Amal Press, 2002).

8. One must agree with the intelligent observation that what threatens the United States nowadays is not "fanatical Islam" but other forces:

> In the face of darkening global conditions and its own transigent post-bubble recession, the real threat to the US today comes not from a handful of Wahhabi fanatics but from Japan's deflating economy. The process of decay, now gathering momentum, risks triggering an implosion that could suck in the the entire region, if not the globe. Gavan McCormack, "Breaking the Iron Triangle." *New Left Review*, Number 13 (January/February, 2002), 5.

    See also Paul Berman, "Al-Qaeda's Philosopher: How an Egyptian Islamist Invented the Terrorist Jihād from his Jail Cell," *New York Times Magazine*, March 23, 2003.

9. For a disappointing analysis of Islamism, see John L. Esposito, *Unholy War: Terror in the Name of Islam* (New York: Oxford University Press, 2002). For a critical review of this book, see Ibrahim M. Abu-Rabi', "John Esposito's *Unholy War*," *The Muslim World*, volume 92 (3 and 4), Fall, 2002: 494–500.

10. See Ibrahim M. Abu-Rabi', *Intellectual Origins of Islamic Resurgence in the Modern Arab World* (Albany: State University of New York Press, 1996).

11. The Lebanese novelist Elias Khury says that the 1967 defeat represented a three-fold absence in Arab thought: (1) absence of consciousness; (2) absence of planning; and (3) absence of the self. See Elias Khury, "al-Nakbah wa'l sira' 'ala al-kalimat." *Al-Tariq*, volume 57(3), May–June, 1998, 4–9.

12. Ghassan Kanafani, "Thoughts on Change and the 'Blind Language'," in Ferial J. Ghazoul and Barbara Harlow, eds., *The View from Within: Writers and Critics on Contemporary Arabic Literature* (Cairo: American University of Cairo Press, 1994), 43.

13. Tharwat 'Ukashah, *Mudhakarat fi'l thaqafah wa'l siyassah*, volume 2 (Cairo: Dar al-Hilāl, 1990), 375.

14. Yassin al-Hafiz, *al-Hazimah wa'l idiulujiyyah al-mahz mah* (Beirut: Dar al-Tali'ah, 1979).

15. Sadiq Jalal al-'Azm, *al-Naqd al-dhati ba'dah al-hazimah* (Beirut: Dar al-Tali'ah, 1969). 'Azm contends that defeat had something to do with the nature of the Arab personality, which is *fahlawi* in nature, a syndrome which, in the words of Fouad Moughrabi, "is related to what others have called the

'lack of reality testing' among the Arabs." Fouad Moughrabi, "The Arabic Basic Personality: A Critical Survey of the Literature," *International Journal of Middle East Studies*, volume 9(1), February, 1978, 104.

16. Sadiq Jalal al-'Azm, *Naqd al-fikr al-dini* (Beirut: Dar al-Tali'ah, 1969).

17. Abdallah Laroui, *L'idéologie arabe contemporaine* (Paris: Maspero, 1970).

18. Yusuf al-Qaradawi, *al-Hall al-islami, faridah wa darurah* (Beirut: Mu'assassat al-Risalah, 1989).

19. Costantine Zurayk, *Ma'nah al-nakbah mujaddadan*, in *al-A'mal al-fikriyyah al-'ammah li Custantine Zurayk*, volume 2 (Beirut: Markaz Dirasat al-Wihdah al-'Arabiyyah, 1994).

20. See Sayyid Yassin, *al-Shakhs iyyah al-'arabiyyah bayna surat al-dhat wa mafhum al-akhar* (Cairo: Maktabat Madbuli, 1993).

21. On this, see Mohammed Haykal, *Autumn of Fury: The Assassination of Sadat*, tr. André Deutsch (London 1983).

22. See also Ayman al-Zawahiri, *al-Hasad al-murr: al-Ikhwan al-Muslimun fi sitin 'am* (Dar al-Bayariq, 2002).

23. John K. Cooley, *Unholy Wars: Afghanistan, America and International Terrorism*, second edition (London: Pluto Press, 2000), 1–3. According to Cooley, the CIA took an active role in recruiting and training different *mujāhideen* groups in Afghanistan:

> The CIA would be the overall manager. US Special Forces and a coalition of assorted allied specialists would train the trainers. Pakistan's ISI, in its schools and camps, would train the bulk of the Moujāhideen and send them into battle; often though not under the same kind of ISI supervision applied to the distribution of weapons. (*Ibid.*, 81)

24. *Ibid.*, 247 (italics added).

Chapter 1

1. Qamari was a contemporary of Zawahiri, who became a military officer with the intention of staging a coup from within the Egyptian Armed Forces. Zawahiri eventually betrayed Qamari's whereabouts under torture, leading to his execution by the Egyptian army.

2. An affluent neighborhood in Cairo, known for its large expatriate community.

3. Literally "calling", meaning that at this time Islamists were active in calling other Egyptians to a life guided by Islamic orthodoxy.

4. 'Abdel 'Azeez was recruited by Zawahiri and also had an important impact on his ideas. He left Egypt with Zawahiri in 1985.

5. *Jihādi* groups are those which believe that violent means should be employed against regimes which do not implement Islamic *shari'a*, and against supporters of such regimes.

6. A member of the Zomor family from Nahia, a poor village style neighborhood near Cairo, 'Abbūd was an officer in the Egyptian Military Intelligence.

7. This group grew out of the union of Zawahiri's group and several other *jihādi* groups operating under various leaders. It was originally called the Jihad Organization. It is also known as the Jihad Group or Egyptian Islamic Jihad (to distinguish it from its Palestinian counterpart also called Islamic Jihad or Palestinian Islamic Jihad). Further mentions of Islamic Jihad in the text refer to the organization founded by Zawahiri in Afghanistan.

8. In Afghanistan, *jihādi* groups established camps for training members to fight the Soviet occupation of the country.

9. In this case, more than 100 members of Islamic Jihad were tried together, many of whom were arrested in Albania and brought home to trial. During the proceedings of this trial, Zawahiri was sentenced to death in absentia.

10. Founded in 1928, the Muslim Brotherhood is among the earliest organizations in Egypt to advocate overthrowing the secular regime. Though it began as a militant group, it has become one of the more moderate contemporary Islamist voices.

11. Also called the Egyptian Delta, Lower Egypt is the fertile Nile valley land along the branches of the Nile that flow north of Cairo.

12. Upper Egypt, also known as the Sa'eed is the fertile land of the Nile valley to the south of Cairo.

13. Poor neighborhoods on the outskirts of Cairo.

14. Raheel was one of Sadāt's assassins.

15. The oldest religious university in the world, Al-Azhar is the central institution for Sunni learning. It also includes schools of modern sciences, arts and humanities.

16. A huge and densely populated neighborhood in Cairo, Shubra is home to a diverse population, but is known for its working-class inhabitants.

17. Fought in 1973, the October War resulted in the signing of a peace treaty with Israel in exchange for the return of the Sinai Peninsula to Egypt. This made Sadat the first Arab leader to recognize the state of Israel. The move was unpopular among Islamists, and was among their motives for his assassination.

18. A region in Upper Egypt.

19. The military courts in Egypt were used as a component of the state of emergency law, or martial law, that was put into effect following the assassination of Sadat, and which remains in effect until today. The military courts

differ from Egyptian civilian courts in several ways: Any accused must be called to trial by a presidential decree; also, verdicts are delivered quickly and are not subject to any appeal process. For this reason, military court verdicts are not recognized by most European countries, and have allowed many Egyptians to win asylum abroad.

20. The State Security courts follow emergency law procedures as do the military courts, except that the accused can be brought to trial without a presidential decree.

21. In 1967, the Egyptian Army fought beside Syrians and Jordanians against the Israeli Army. The war led to a demoralizing defeat and the Israeli seizure and occupation of parts of all three countries.

22. Egyptian president known for his charismatic leadership of the Pan-Arabist movement and for his efforts to modernize Egypt through socialist reorganization of the economy.

23. Student organizations in Egyptian Universities organize summer camps and retreats to draw students with various interests. Islamist students organized summer retreats including conferences and activities to promote Islamic *da'wa* at the university.

24. City in upper Egypt.

25. In Islamic *shari'a*, a Muslim leader has to be able to see in order to be capable of performing his duties.

Chapter 2

1. A new suburb of Cairo, home to the Monument of the Unknown Soldier where the celebration of the October War victory was held.

2. Members of the Gamā'a al-Islāmiyya killed 58 tourists of various nationalities as well as four Egyptians in the Temple of Queen Hatshepsut in Luxor. Group leaders announced after the incident that they intended only to take hostages to convince the United States to release their captive leader Sheikh 'Abdel Rahmān.

3. Vanguards of Conquest is a splinter group of Islamic Jihad established by Ahmed Hussein 'Ogayza after he broke away over a disagreement with Zawahiri. In 1995, the arrest of dozens of its members led to four cases in which 42 people were convicted for belonging to the group.

4. A low-income neighborhood in Cairo.

5. A graduate of Al-Azhar University.

6. In August of 1998, a truck bomb planted outside the US Embassy in Nairobi exploded at the same time as another outside the US Embassy in Darussalam. The attacks killed more than 200 people and injured thousands. The United

States brought four men accused of having links to Al-Qaeda to trial for the attacks and sentenced them to life imprisonment.

7. Two men in a small boat drove a bomb into the American destroyer *Cole* in the Aden port in Yemen in October of 2000, killing several American sailors, and severely damaging one side of the ship.

8. Meaning "pyramids", this area is part of Greater Cairo, but is officially in Giza near the Great Pyramids. The area is home to low-income neighborhoods as well as flashy hotels and the city's most well known belly-dancing clubs.

9. These security forces, charged with the personal safety of the president, are the best-trained and equipped security forces in the country.

10. Low-income neighborhood in Cairo.

11. Low-income neighborhood in Cairo.

12. Low-income neighborhood in Cairo.

13. In 1965, the Nasser regime cracked down on the Muslim Brotherhood imprisoning many of its members and hanging Sayyid Qutb.

14. Taliban: the Taliban, meaning "students", was one of the many *mujāhideen* groups struggling for control of Afghanistan after the Soviet withdrawal from the country in 1989. The largely Pashtun group seized control from President Burhanuddin Rabbani in 1996. It was known for its strict Islamist rule of the country and for giving refuge to Osāma bin Lāden.

15. The accused were arrested for planning to blow up a group of Israeli tourists in Khān al-Khalili, a famous market in Cairo frequented by tourists looking for oriental souvenirs.

16. The four imāms are the thinkers who founded the four great canonical schools of thought in Islamic *fiqh*. Zawahiri here means that the group subscribes to a traditional Sunni philosophy, not an extremist or fringe philosophy.

17. Literally "Identifying Infidels and Migrating [away from them]" the Takfir wal Hijra group is among the most extreme *jihādi* groups. Its members seek to identify and target Muslim civilians and regimes that do not meet their standards of piousness.

Chapter 3

1. At this time, Afghan militias were fighting the Soviet occupation of the country. Muslims from other countries joined them in what they saw as a struggle against the forced secularization of the Communist empire.

2. Independent London-based Arabic language newspaper.

3. The 1993 attempt to bomb the minister's motorcade from in front of the American University in Cairo resulted in the death of both assassins, but did not kill the minister.

4. In 1993, a car belonging to the then prime minister 'Atef Sidqi was blown up in front of his home. While he was not killed, the explosion accidentally killed a child named Shayma'. A bystander was also later assassinated because he had witnessed the crime.

Chapter 4

1. "Opened" here means coming under Muslim control. The term is a reference to the Arab conquests in the time of the Prophet.
2. This and all following citations from the Koran are as translated and interpreted by Muhammad Taqi-ud-Din Al-Hilâlî and Muhammad Muhsin Khân, *Interpretation of the Meanings of the Noble Qur'an in the English Language* (Riyadh: Maktaba Darussalam, 1997), At-Tawba (11:123).
3. In April of 1996, several Greek tourists were mistaken for Israelis and were gunned down outside the Europa Hotel on the road to visit the pyramids.
4. A university in Upper Egypt.

Chapter 5

1. High level decision-making body in Islamic organizations and governments, which takes decisions through consensus.
2. Meaning "he who has preformed the obligatory pilgrimage", the term "hajj" is used commonly as a title of respect for one senior in age or status.
3. *Qur'an,* Al-Hijr (14:47).
4. Literally "prince," refers in the text to the leader of an Islamist group.
5. The term "imām" for Sunnis refers to a religious person responsible for leading prayers in the mosque. Here "Great Imām" refers to the leader of the greater Muslim *umma,* or the caliph.
6. *Qur'an,* Al-Burûj (30:10).

Chapter 6

1. In June of 1996, a truck bomb drove into the dormitory complex of the Al-Khubar Towers in Saudi Arabia, killing 19 American servicemen.
2. Cities in Upper Egypt.
3. After the September 11, 2001 attacks on the United States, the bank was put on the Bush administration's list of organizations suspected of financing terrorist groups. Shareholders include several prominent individuals from numerous Middle Eastern countries.

Chapter 8

1. *Qur'an*, Âl-'Imrân (4:165).
2. *Qur'an*, Al-Mâ'idah (6:54).
3. *Qur'an*, Al-Anfâl (9:15–16).
4. *Qur'an*, Al-Anfâl (9:25).
5. *Qur'an*, Al-Anfâl (9:24).
6. *Qur'an*, An-Nisâ (5:65).
7. *Qur'an*, Ar-Ra'd (13:33).
8. *Qur'an*, Al-Anfâl (10:63).
9. *Qur'an* Az-Zumar (24:53).
10. Famous Arabian warrior and folk hero.

Index